HOW TO SUCCEED IN THE BLOCKCHAIN AND BITCOIN 2022

Beginner's Guide to Earning Money as an Investor

CONTENTS

IF YOU DON'T UNDERSTAND THE INFINITE GAME YOU'LL BELIEVE THE BITCOIN NETWORK WILL FALL

HOW ETHEREUM WILL RESHAPE AND TOKENIZE ENTIRE SECTORS OF OUR ECONOMY

HOW TOKENS WILL BUILD POLITICAL ENLIGHTENING COMMUNITIES ALL OVER THE WORLD

IT'S NOT THE CORPORATIONS THAT WILL HOLD THE POWER IN THE FUTURE, BUT COMMUNITIES OR TOKENS

Introduction

This ebook is not deep research work, as I am not a Ph.D. professor at any international university.

I was a teacher. I was also a real estate investor. And now I am a fulltime writer. Nevertheless, I am also research addicted reading two books per month.

Moreover, as I studied Macroeconomics, I found out that the world has been threatened by a new virus, the decentralized digital virus.

Metaverse, Decentraland, blockchain, bitcoin standard, smart contracts, protocols, nodes, tokens, and halvings suddenly invaded my eyes with such a power that I had to understand what the hell was that about.

If you do not know what these concepts are, you are in the right place.

Some of these articles are controversial, others you might agree with, but most of them try to explain how the world is shifting into a fully digital mode.

Central banks and governments are trying to keep the boat afloat in a perfect MMT style, while politicians still do not quite understand how the money-printing machine works. They keep saying we need raise taxes to pay the debt when the government is the only issuer, so it cannot become insolvent.

With deflationary pressure from technological innovations, the need for fresh money puts central banks in the red to control inflation.

Covid-19 hit hard on every economy, but only the issuers can control the orchestra.

Straightforwardly, as a non-native writer, I will try to give you a perspective about how the world is changing, from analog to digital, from the real world to the metaverse, with a fascinating silent war between centralized money printing power and decentralized fully digital crypto ecosystems.

PART I: THE MACRO

HOW DID WE BREAK CAPITALISM

Adam Smith's vision puts people first.

I recently wrote an article where I talk about the lack of morality of the current financial system and how it can have a destructive effect on the behavioral trust process of human beings.

Milton Friedman, in the 1990s, defended the logic of putting the shareholder's desires ahead of the customer or the employee.

We argue that Friedman's economic writings assume an economy in which businesses operate under limited liability protection, which allows corporations to privatize their gains while externalizing their losses. By accepting limited liability, Friedman must also view business as embedded in social interdependency, which serves as the logical and moral foundation for corporate social responsibility (CSR).- Ignacio Ferrero, W. Michael Hoffman, Robert E. McNulty in onlinelibrary.wiley.com

This was the first step to the loss of morality in the financial system. We now see where it all went for; Jeff Bezos buying a multi-billiondollar yacht and so many other extravaganzas.

Lack of morality can destroy an entire country or economy, but something scarier can also happen- the rise of radical leaders such as Adolf Hitler, Mussolini, or Stalin: those who promised to moralize the political system with moralized politics, remember?

There's nothing wrong with capitalism, except that we've broken it.

Capitalism is Adam Smith's vision where he puts people first.

No society can surely be flourishing and happy, of which the far more significant part of the members are poor and miserable.- Adam Smith

But what happened to capitalism? What did we do wrong? How did we manage to get to this point?

People don't buy what you do; they buy why you do it.

We have been playing with the wrong rules for a long time.

Not like a game rule, but economic rules. According to James P. Carse, we have finite and infinite games when playing games, but also when we're at our jobs.

A finite game is defined with a certain number of players, fixed rules, and a finite goal, like soccer. There are referees to control the rules, and in a defined time frame, whoever gets more points wins the game. There's a beginning, a middle, and an end.

And then, there's the infinite game. An infinite game is defined as known and unknown players; new players can join at any time, the game has changeable rules, and the goal is to perpetuate the game- to stay in the game as long as possible.

Marriage is an infinite game; you can't say you have won a marriage. You wouldn't know who won global politics or won in a business.

Yet, if you watch some leaders talking about success, they say things like be the number one, be the best, or beat their competition.

Based on what?

There are no metrics on winning a marriage or a business. If you try to win marriage, you'd no longer be married. If you'd try to win a business, you wouldn't know when it ends, so it would be at least awkward.

In other words, people are playing the infinite game with a finite mindset. And if you're playing the same game with the wrong rules, something happens- the decline of trust, the decline of cooperation, and the decline of innovation.

Simon Sinek, author of the book Start With Why: How Great Leaders Inspire

Everyone To Take Action, spoke at an educational summit at Microsoft and at Apple.

At the Microsoft summit, most executives spend most of their time talking about how to beat Apple.

At the Apple summit, a hundred percent of their executives spend all their time talking about how they could help teachers teach and how to get help students to learn.

One was obsessed with where they were going, the other was obsessed with beating their competition.

When Elon Musk created SpaceX, he didn't spend his energy thinking about how he could beat Virgin Galactic, Blue Origin, or NASA. Instead, he wanted to build a company to colonize Mars and found a way to do it. Elon Musk has an infinite mindset.

———————————— *nf* ————————————

Why the tokenization of the entire economy?

Bitcoin is now formally preparing to be an asset class. It can't be banned shortly neither "criminalized." The Bank for International Settlements proposes differentiating between crypto-assets based on the market, liquidity, credit, and operational risks.

Today, the Basel Committee on Banking Supervision issued a public consultation on preliminary proposals for the prudential treatment of banks' crypto-asset exposures. While banks' exposures to cryptoassets are currently limited, the continued growth and innovation in crypto-assets and related services, coupled with the heightened interest of some banks, could increase global financial stability concerns and risks to the banking system in the absence of a specified prudential treatment. - bis.org

Why did the Bitcoin network win after so much disbelief from the mainstream? Because the developers and coders have an infinite mindset.

It all began in 2009 when Satoshi Nakamoto wrote a 9-page white paper where he mentioned:

A purely peer-to-peer version of electronic cash would allow online payments to be sent directly from one party to another without going through a financial institution. Digital signatures provide part of the solution, but the main benefits are lost if a trusted third party is still required to prevent double-spending.- Satoshi Nakamoto in bitcoin.org.

The behavioral incentive to disrupt the monetary system was so powerful that developers and coders wanted it to happen, so they followed Nakamoto's first block of the Bitcoin symbolically named Gemini, into thousands of other blocks in a totally decentralized monetary system that will, I hope, be part of the global financial system.

An all-new industry is being built, at this moment, under a premise of a decentralized system, avoiding third parties to change the rules, in a peer-to-peer protocol philosophy, more transparent, reliable, and trustworthy.

Why did the Bitcoin Network survive all the attempts to its destruction?

The creators started building the system with an infinite mindset, meaning developers and coders knew already what was wrong with the current monetary system and began to build a completely disruptive new system, under the premise of not making the same mistakes governments and central banks did in the past.

The tokenization of the entire financial industry is a reality. New communities will continuingly be created, with different blockchains benefiting protocols that don't need third parties to be functional.

Trustworthy protocols have to be validated in a peer-to-peer relationship for transactions to occur.

Developers and coders didn't want to beat the current financial system; they built another one, completely different from the existing one. In an infinite game, you don't want to beat the competition; you want to solve problems and move one to the next challenge.

The Bitcoin Network and the blockchain were built to solve problems, not to beat the competition. And because of that, governments realized that it can't be destroyed, like Microsoft thought could happen against Apple.

---

nf

How did we break capitalism?

After the 2008 Great Recession, millions of citizens all over the world watched the shameless episode of the banking collapse and the recognition of the existence of a banking elite that not only got away with the greedy engineering created but also returned to the party with the approval of governments and central banks.

We all have short memories, but what happened in 2008 should not only have been a warning; it would have been a golden opportunity to moralize a financial system steeped in greed, lust, and waste.

It didn't happen, though.

The almost romantic story of Satoshi Nakamoto that no one knows who he, she, they are is at least flagship. Even more so when the 9page white paper was created precisely in 2008, after the last financial crisis. And the creation of the Bitcoin Network was neither more nor less to destroy the rotten system that broke out in the great recession.

If governments at that time had dared to take appropriate action, the financial system would have been highly moralized, and perhaps the Bitcoin Network would not have been born, or at least it would have been created under a different premise.

I don't believe central banks will disappear. On the contrary, with the creation of the CBDCs (Central Bank Digital Currency), central bankers will increase their power over citizens and monetize the entire money behavioral actions.

It's going to be a modern socialism kind of political arrangement.

On the other side, a totally decentralized monetary system is arising, built under the premises of individual freedom. At some point, I believe central bankers will try to manipulate the decentralized system, not willing to lose control of the money supply they so carefully manage.

At the end of the road, no one knows what will happen. I hope a more decentralized and moralized system arises, not at the cost of the fragile ones.

Millennials have the power to start the shift, moralizing communities or tokens and building bridges between blockchains and the postindustrial revolution era.

A new industry will arise with the environment behavioral philosophy under their vision and motto. Climate change, renewable energy, decentralized finance, tokenization of the global economy will be premises for millennials to guarantee a moralized and healthier ecosystem for future generations.

Millennials and GenZ know what they have to do, and they are part of the change- they are making the change.

— *MF* —

Final Thoughts

Let me be frank with you- I don't like what central banks have been doing for the last decades.

They constantly benefit the few over the majority. The gap between the rich and the poor is at levels that deter any ordinary citizen from fighting for a supposedly just and equitable democracy.

On the other hand, governments could try to find better solutions to the inequality problem, decentralizing the financial system. I understand that a currency is a geopolitical weapon that saves us from conflicts and wars, but it's also a tool to enrich the few to the detriment of the majority.

Something in between would be the best solution, and I believe it's possible to achieve it. Unfortunately, there will be conflicts between the decentralized Bitcoin Network and the blockchain ecosystem, and the post-industrial revolution economic system.

In this challenging transition, many will fall; others will rise to build the future with climate change, inequality, and abundance as priorities.

Pure infinite gamification of our mindsets.

WHY YOU SHOULD DO EXACTLY THE OPPOSITE GOVERNMENTS WANT YOU TO DO

Beware of little expenses; a small leak will sink a great ship.

Before I turn myself into a full-time writer, I worked in the real estate business.

I made almost $20,000 a year, plus some real estate investments that generally made me earn another 15k. So, I reached nearly a minimum of $35,000 per year, which is very good for a Portuguese.

The minimum wage in Portugal is $715, and the average salary is $1,500.

Yet, if your financial philosophy is to spend all your money in credits, it doesn't matter if your Portuguese, American, English, or Chinese.

In a world where the financial system is structured for you to spend money, if you play the same game as governments want you to play, you'll be running the rat race indefinitely.

What do I mean by that? The banking system was built to create a credit cycle for people to spend money with fees. If you want a house, first, you buy the bank's capital, meaning the bank will lend you money in exchange for commissions.

You get the money upfront, and the bank charges you the interest on that loan. It seems simple, but in this game, if the temptation is too big, we are in a rat race, with loans for the house, car, television, PlayStation, clothes, and so on.

Generally, ordinary people don't save money, so when a financial crisis arrives, they have to give back their house to the bank for someone with money to buy it at a discount. Ordinary people turn to poor people, and the ones who saved money get more prosperous. So it's a vicious cycle.

But why can't ordinary people save money? Because they don't have a proper financial education. They don't know how the money works and how they should manage their income.

The financial system was built for all of us to spend money, not save it.

Even governments spend more money than they earn. That's why you hear that debt is constantly rising. Fortunately, governments and institutions buy the country's debt from one to another until one day this system stops working.

It's much easier for you to lend money that isn't yours and carry the problem to a later time. The problem we have later is that we have to pay back what we borrowed, plus interest.

Apart from the house and eventually the car, everything else should be purchased through savings, but most people reject this strategy.

So, in reality, what is the best plan for managing our lives, creating wealth, and becoming financially independent?

———————————— *nF* ————————————

I had no idea bankruptcy could be so exciting.

At 31 years old, I was bankrupt.

To speak the truth, at 27, I was also bankrupt. So, in 5 year-time, I was bankrupted twice, but for different reasons.

As you can imagine, being without any money to support my family and bringing food to the table is very dramatic to a young adult.

Yet, it was the only way I could learn. I had the worst financial education anyone could have. And this lesson cost me $32,000 that I had to pay smoothly in small amounts every month for the next 8 years.

Now, I'm proudly credit-free, and I have enough money to breathe, live, and appreciate compounding interests.

In the learning process that cost me $32,000 (2 bankruptcies), I read all the books I needed about financial independence. I read Warren Buffett, Howard Marks, Peter Lynch, and even Tony Robbins.

My father always said that Everything is in the books.

And he was right! As I was in my learning process, I realized that the same person that gave me the worst financial education, my father, also gave me the best solution.

My father always believed that commercial banks and their workers could help me when I needed money. But what my father didn't know was that when you rely only on credit, one day you'll get hung up and then begin the rat race again.

Only books could teach me how to manage money.

Put all your eggs in one basket, and then watch that basket.

When I was in my learning process to stop being a rat racer and become a free man, I read a simple book that changed my life.

The author of that book was a young and entrepreneur Portuguese guy that explained in the simplest way possible how money works and how anyone can escape the rat race and have enough money to feel free.

The book was called My First Million.

For the first time, I heard someone talking about the Dream Basket. But what is the dream basket, after all?

Imagine you close your eyes and start dreaming about things you would love to have or to do. Now, write them on a piece of paper. Next, put the amount of money you need to fulfill those dreams and at what age you think you can satisfy them. Then, add it all up and see the result.

Dream basket

Everything starts with a dream.

Do you want to be in the same house 10 years from now? Then, finally, you want to make that memorable trip for three months? Do you want to quit your 9 to 5 tedious job?

Ignore all your fears and allow yourself to dream.

Dreams get people close to each other and get all strengths together.

Creating a simple task of designing a dream basket change immediately our mindset. Our subconscious starts an automatic process of finding intelligent ways to reach the set goals.

With perseverance and patience, anyone can see their dream basket full of good things in a strict savings regime.

I found out that I need 2.5 million dollars to get what I want.

One of my dreams was to buy a farm, plant as many trees as possible, export wild berries, and whatever profit I'll make, donate it to Scott Harrison's foundation, Charity Water, which supplies water pumps to offer clean water to villages in Africa and Asia.

785 million human beings lack clean water, causing 18,000 child deaths due to food shortages and disease.

I already bought the farm. Now I'm in the rebuilding process, and I have started planting trees. At the end of the year, I'm beginning the wild barriers project.

Another dream in my basket is to travel all over the world. Planet earth is the most precious and beautiful thing any human being has.
I'd love to know it better.

And that's it.

My dream basket is short and straightforward.

I live in Europe, a prosperous continent. In Portugal, I have everything most people would love to have. I'm a privileged human being, but most human beings are not. And there are so many things to do on that behalf.

Do not save what is left after spending, but spend what is left after saving.

Read that headline again.

Pay yourself first. Pay yourself first. Pay yourself first.

Can you put 10% of your income in a savings account? Can you put 20%, or 30%?

As much you save, the closer you are to fulfill your dreams. Yet, if you want to save what is left after spending, you're not hearing what Warren Buffett is whispering at your ear.

My car has 18 years old and I'm in a renting house. I just buy clothes when it's indispensable. Yet, if you see my banking account, I may be considered a wealthy guy.

Why don't I change to a new car? Why don't I buy a new house?

I could do both without needing a loan. But that was not what Warren Buffett taught me to do.

I'm accumulating my savings, investing them to make the magic formula work for me. And the magic formula is called **compound interests.**

I invest every month a portion of my savings in the stock market and another part in the real estate business.

I have a life with controlled costs so that one day I can achieve financial independence. But, for that, I can't spend what I don't have.

On the contrary, I pay myself first; that is, as soon as I receive my salary, I put 30% aside in savings and live with the 70% left over. This 70% does not allow me to buy a new car or a new house. I learned that this is the magic formula for achieving my financial independence.

I will have to be able to have a fixed monthly income to cover my fixed expenses. Only then will I be truly free and have the money working for me.

—————————— *NF* ——————————

Final Thoughts

After you finish this article, you'll find it challenging to change your mindset into a saving mindset. Believe me, I've been there. I was bankrupted twice, remember?

If you really want to do something, you'll find a way. If you don't, you'll find an excuse.- Jim Rohn

What is your little devil whispering in your ear right now?

The little devil is probably saying nobody understands your life. The little devil is saying that you can't do it because of this or because of that.

You can make an infinite list of reasons why you can't be financially independent. My subconscious spoke to me 15 years ago and said the same to me too.

See, we have this selfish way to manage our own interests. And generally, we want to take the shorter cut. We don't want it to hurt or take too long.

Just like starting a workout after being in a pure sedentary lifestyle for decades, changing our mindset to something painful it's not an easy task. And not everyone can overcome their own inertia.

Those who manage to overcome all the traps our mindsets do to us are the lucky ones.

Those who continue to listen to the little devil continue to feel that the government, friends, family, dog, cat, or parrot are to blame for their ineffectiveness.

The power is all in our minds.

THE CATASTROPHIC ADDICTION CENTRAL BANKS HAVE TO PRINT ENORMOUS AMOUNTS OF MONEY

Why it's going to be so hard to embrace abundance.

Why don't we pay money to use the air we breathe?

If air is the most valuable thing on earth, why don't you pay for it? Because it's abundant.

We're living in an era of abundance creation because of technology disruption. Meaning, innovation is taking prices cheaper, almost free.

Innovation is also taking our jobs, so we need fewer jobs because robots are doing it more efficiently and costly.

Abundance is taking place. However, for the abundant system to emerge, the old system will have to collapse.

What will be the consequences, and what is happening now that we can't clearly see this massively colossal shift from the old system to the new system?

—————————— *NF* ——————————

He who is quick to borrow is slow to pay.

Accordingly to one of the most respectful hedge fund managers, Ray Dalio, there are only four ways governments can escape debt crisis:

- Austerity- spending less
- Debt defaults/restructuring
- The central bank printing money or other guarantees
- Transfers of money from those who have more than they need to those who have less (much higher taxes for the rich)

Whether starting with austerity or restructuring, both would create a vicious cycle of asset prices collapse, combined with lower employment. It is the most painful government tool to the society in the short term. That's probably why this kind of dialogue is not shared in the public sphere.

Central banks printing money, combined with a low or negative interest rate environment, ironically, makes us believe in a free market and capitalism, but if you deeply think about it, that's not what is happening in the real world.

The only conclusion we can make on money printing and lowering interest rate policies is that it keeps the party going by driving more debt.

From a macroeconomic perspective, driving more debt only pushes the pain in the longer term.

In the shorter term, it only makes successful people feel wealthier.

You can see it by what happened in the Great Recession of 2008. Governments took place, bought the problems with printing money, the reaches kept their parties on, and the world moved on.

All of this happened with half a dozen people arrested, with most of the leading players being surgically placed in different positions, but the group of friends remained the same for the party to continue.

It's like you have a group of people rearranging the Titanic chairs while the boat keeps sinking.

The Federal Reserve is printing 120 billion dollars per month to keep the boat afloat. One day will come, probably sooner than we think, when our heads are underwater, and we can't hear the music playing anymore.

Once bondholders determine that governments have little ability to repay or service the debt, the risk premium (or interest rates) on the debt will rise. Sure, governments can monetize and make their currencies worthless, but as other central banks monetize as well, the strategy itself becomes irrelevant. Jeff Booth in The Price of Tomorrow

This mischievous game has only one endgame: higher inequality, people losing hope in the system, more polarization, the rise of radical leaders, and lastly, revolutions or war.

The problem with socialism is that you eventually run out of other peoples' money.

There are no perfect systems.

Socialism goes by the principle that the system should be fair to the disadvantage. However, if we increase the tax rates on the wealthy, the more disincentives they have to produce innovation and jobs and be strong contributors to society.

With more jobs being destroyed by innovation and money being printed out of thin air, recent Universal Basic Income (UBI) proposals are beginning to take shape.

The idea is simple: tax the rich to support people who have no jobs.
In theory, this sounds reasonable, even for the most fervent capitalists. Why? Because in a world with zero consumption, capitalism also dies.

Yet, if you turn an economy to fewer and fewer participants, the math doesn't work anyway, and the system will also collapse.

UBI is pernicious in its essence. It discourages innovation and wealth creation, showing that people do not need to work because someone will do it for them. Then, we also have the problem of the 'fair' value been given to each citizen, in each country, each city, or state.

Ultimately, the Universal Basic Income would not solve the root cause.

Deflation is not being caused by bad people from central banks or governments. I believe they are trying to do their best to keep things going.

Deflation is being caused by technology disruption.

This means the tsunami caused by deflationary innovation will keep pressure on global economies. The abundance that technology provides to the humanity does not need more jobs. On the contrary, it replaces employment with more efficient and cheaper solutions.

This negative effect on jobs will only accelerate over the next few decades.

Ignoring this simple concept will only make the world more divided, less globalized, unequal, and permissive to populism, divisionism, and conflict.

—————————————— *nF* ——————————————

To survive, our economy must work with nature, not against it — time to reset.

All governments are trying to print into this problem because the system requires it.

If you would allow the free market to take place, you'd have a deflationary spiral. Yet, the debt is so large, and everybody owns debt- governments, corporations, companies, and individuals- with absolutely nothing backing it. It's only counterparty risks all the way down.

Meaning, if you allow the debt spiral to take place, everything on top of debt will fail, including governments, banks, institutions, hospitals, everything.

Why does it look that bad? It looks horrible because it breaks the natural rules of the free market. Mother nature comes in cycles. You can't stop winter from going after fall. So, trying to stop recessions hoping you can grow forever is insane. That's not how the free market works.

From a government's perspective, they have 4 years cycles, and it's more convenient for politicians to find easy and short-term ways to make the population feel wealthy. And because of that, they try to control inflation at all costs.

The problem is not from the right or the left, the republicans or democrats; it's about the system and the debt cycles. That's their natural order, and trying to fight against it, is simply suicide.

The more you fight nature, free market, and technology, the more you increase the bubbles and pass to future generations a bigger problem. Politicians know that, but they cannot fight it because they genuinely want to be elected.

So, we start to see signs of very experiment politics suggesting a reset:

The Great Reset agenda would have three main components. The first would steer the market toward fairer outcomes. To this end, governments should improve coordination (for example, in tax, regulatory, and fiscal policy), upgrade trade arrangements, and create the conditions for a "stakeholder economy." At a time of diminishing tax bases and soaring public debt, governments have a powerful incentive to pursue such action.- Klaus Schwab, founder and Executive Chairman of World Economic Forum.

──────────── *nf* ────────────

Abundance is not something we acquire. It is something we tune into.

The simple solution is far from simple.

Occam's razor philosophy says that a simple solution is more likely to be correct than a complex one.

In this particular case that we live in, it seems the complex solution is only postponing the painful decision to embrace abundance.

It's almost like having a cut on the finger and wanting to remove the dressing, but we are postponing the moment just to postpone those few seconds of pain.

The problematic and straightforward question is: what if the natural order of things was permitted? What if, instead of trying to fight deflation at all costs, we embrace it?

If everything- not just phones or Internet companies but EVERYTHING- is giving far more performance and at the same time falling in price, a family that makes $75,000 this year and struggles to make ends meet could make $70,000 next year and the dollars would go further. And then $60,000 a few years after that and it would go further still, continuing to gain more for less with the natural deflationary trend in technology. That would allow us to step off the existing treadmill of chasing higher and higher prices, requiring even higher-paying jobs to keep up.

That may sound radical, but if technology is deflationary, and we expect technology to continue its advance into more and more industries, it may not be radical at all. It may be the only sane thing to do.- Jeff Booth in The Price of Tomorrow

—————————————— *nF* ——————————————

Final Thoughts

Governments all over the world are in a genuine rat race. They keep printing money to control inflation and employment, but they can't fight technology innovation.

The only rational solution is the hardest one, embracing the natural order of things and letting deflation take its place.

However, no politician will be able to embrace deflation because it would mean losing power. So, we're facing an endless road.

A great reset is already taking place, but a new agreement like Bretton Wood 2.0 is required. And the borrowers are the ones who are going to be wiped out.

Debts can't and will not be paid because countries can't provide sufficient growth to pay them. It's simple math.

And central banks can't monetize everything eternally. But governments will not voluntarily give up control of their currencies. So, it has to happen a coordinated international effort to establish new rules around money.

Currencies only hold value because of the trust we have in them.

Trust is increasing in the Bitcoin network, as it spread all over the world, as a possible finite asset collateralizing a new entire financial sector.

If governments do not keep their promises, the more trust eroded, the more likely alternative currencies become more trusted.

It's clear that something has to be done, but the complex system we live in is not seeing what is happening. And what is happening is that a new system is taking place, with code and cryptography as the trust entity, not humans.

Technology disruption is taking place in the financial industry. But most politicians keep thinking that their complicity with central banks, commercial banks, and powerful institutions gives them a bulletproof vest.

If you know history, you have endless examples of the quick fashion way technology disruptions take place. Just remember what the combustion engine did to city landscapes or what the electricity did to our modern way of living.

Somehow, somewhere, silently, technology disruptions always win.

THE MONEY RESET HAS ALREADY BEGUN: SHOCKING DETAILS

The Great Reset broke into 4 sections.

It's the right thing to do. It's time to reinvent capitalism postcoronavirus.- Doug McMillon, Walmart's CEO

For most people, money history is a boring theme.

So rest assured, I won't bother you with storytelling on how a native from a remote island exchanged goods with his neighbor.

Halfway there, you'd been asleep, anyway.

I will shorten the path and explain to you, in four points, how the world will turn upside down its entire monetary system.

If you know how to be on the right side, you'll benefit first.

———————————— *NF* ————————————

1) How It Was Created The First Fake Money

England needed money to defeat the French. In 1694 the British came from a civil war so that the English king couldn't raise more money. At that time, the richest were the bankers and England's credit was terrible.

So a committee of the House of Commons was formed. Sir William Paterson suggested a new scheme for the parliament.

In return for the parliament to give particular privileges, Paterson and a wealthy elite created the Bank of England.

Bank of England could issue new paper notes and use them to finance the English deficit.

The bank gave particular privileges to those who could create money out of thin air.

Sounds familiar?

When England decided to print money out of thin air, what do you think the rest of the world did? Right. They started to print money as well.

Fiat currency refers to any money that a government declares to be legal tender. The cycle of fiat currencies rises and collapses — almost every time due to inflation and devaluation.

It starts with the printing money injected into the economy. All this new money creates an economic boom.

Yet, over time, because of human nature, it becomes overprinted. Because it's overprinted, it starts to create inflation. Then it starts losing value and it devalues enough to lead to its collapse.

What comes after that?

The game has to be reset.

———————————— *nf* ————————————

2) Setting Up The Great Reset

There are no historical precedents of a fiat currency that had succeeded in holding its value.

The average life expectancy for a fiat currency is only 27 years.

There are some exceptions. The British pound sterling has been around for more than 300 years. However, over its 300 years of history, this fiat currency lost over 99,5% of its value.

The US dollar is the world's reserve currency since the Nixon shock. While Nixon's actions did not formally abolish the existing Bretton Woods international financial exchange system, the suspension of one of its key components effectively rendered the Bretton Woods system inoperative.

Nixon did unilaterally step out of the Bretton Woods agreement in 1971. Fifty years later, the dollar is blowing up. It seems that the US dollar has exceeded in 23 years the average life expectancy of a fiat currency.

Currencies always blow up the same way.

In September 2019, the repo markets collapsed. The big banks knocked at the Fed's door, asking it to substitute as a lender at rates they would consider normal, that is, about 2%. The Fed hesitated for a moment before massively intervening by injecting over 50 billion dollars of liquidity on 17 September 2019.

I could give other examples, but the game goes on and on.

Jeff Booth said that,

It took $185 trillion of debt to produce about $45 trillion of GDP growth over the last twenty years.- Jeff Booth in The Price of Tomorrow

After the repo market short crisis, the Fed was wading into the breach, firing the "big bazookas" of monetary policy, pumping trillions of dollars into the world's giant pool of money.

When you have the central banks telling you that this was because of the pandemic, it's not true.

The pandemic represents a rare but narrow window of opportunity to reflect, reimagine, and reset our world — Professor Klaus Schwab, Founder, and Executive Chairman, World Economic Forum.

The great reset is close, and there is a strong possibility of all central banks embracing this unique opportunity- the pandemic's excuse- to reset the system.

Some think central banks want to save the system.

What if they don't want to save the system? What if they're waiting for the perfect time to make the shift?

———————— $\mathcal{NF}$ ————————

3) What Does It Look Like On The Other Side?

Probably it's the end of currency as we know it.

We're not going to have money or currency again. We're going to have CBDCs, also called digital fiat currency or digital base money.

It's going to be a government ledger — a credit system.

In 2018, a BIS survey, the Bank of International Settlements, which "fosters international monetary and financial cooperation and serves as a bank for central banks," reported that 63 central banks were already working on a digital currency.

China was the first one to release its CBDC. Other countries are pretty close to following the Chinese, like Sweden, Turkey, Iran, or Argentina. In fact, the USA is working hard on its cryptocurrency.

The IMF, International Monetary Fund, by the name of Christine Lagarde, as recently reported,

Let us consider the possibility of issuing digital currency. There may be a role for the state to supply money to the digital economy.

This currency could satisfy public policy goals, such as (i) financial inclusion and (ii) security and consumer protection; and to provide what the private sector cannot: (iii) privacy in payments.

We're witnessing the beginning of the big reset. Shifting from the currency system over to a digital form of currency.

Yet, this is not money as we know it. It's something completely different.

Money, we can hold ourselves. We can have access to cash, and we can exchange with each other, or even keep it at home.

CBDCs are different entities. **It's programmable money**. When central banks give it out, they can program it to do certain things. For example, they can program a certain amount of money and say to you if you don't spend it until Friday, it will return to us.

Central banks will have the power to force you to spend their money whenever they want. They can also shift it to change your behavior. How can it happen?

Central banks will encourage you to save or spend digital money by charging a fee or paying interest. It will depend, as you spend or save, within a framework that they will define.

Don't panic. These fiscal 'stimulus' already happen in the current economy. Governments charge fees or pay interest as they intend to model your behavior.

The big difference between the present monetary system and the CBDC system is that you could save your money at home or do whatever you wanted with it.

CBDC system will work with credits, and you'll have credits to spend. You will earn credits, and you will use those credits.

The thing is, CBDCs are going to control and surveil the entire system, and that's a scary world.

The future is still a project design. These are presumptions based on the information we have available today.

———————————— $n\mathcal{F}$ ————————————

4) Surviving The Great Currency Reset

The best way not to be caught in this game is not to play the game at all.

Owning real and tangible assets is the only way of being out of the system- own real wealth. Money is not wealth. Money measures wealth.

Wealth is real hard assets, like gold, silver, or Bitcoin.

The difference between gold and Bitcoin is that BTC is not a physical entity. But unlike gold, which can increase due to mining production, BTC has a protocol of 21 million digital coins. So, it cannot be inflated or manipulated.

Holding our purchasing power outside the system will be the ultimate goal.

We should have total independence of the central banks' control.

The dollar is losing 10 to 15% of its value, year after year. So everybody who owns gold is not riding the ascending wave they aspire.

As gold increases its values, miners also increase their production. That is, gold becomes less scarce. It is losing value. Besides, gold buyers need more dollars to buy it. Hence, in reality, gold is not valuing at the speed that people think it is.

According to supply and demand, as the number of BTCs is finite, 21 million of them will value or devalue. There's no external entity manipulating the system.

If you think that secrecy from governments and no KYC is bitcoins future, you don't understand what adoption looks like. They will regulate it. You will declare it. You will have to do KYC, and that is fine. It doesn't take away its store of value but just integrates it.-
Raoul Pal from realvision.com

———————————— *nF* ————————————

Final Thoughts

If you want to understand the debt cycles and how monetary systems work, you should read what Ray Dalio has been sharing on LinkedIn.

There are four levers that policymakers can pull to bring debt and service levels down to income and cash flows that are required to service them:

1- Austerity- spending less;
2- Debt defaults/restructuring;
3- The central bank printing money or other guarantees;
4- Transfers of money from those who have more than they need to those who have less (much higher taxes for the rich).

Dalio concludes that in the end, "Policymakers always print. That is because austerity causes more pain than benefit, big restructurings wipe out too much wealth too fast, and transfers of wealth from the haves to have nots don't happen in sufficient size without revolution." Dalio studied 5,000 years of rising and falling of all the great empires.

He studied the debt cycles and realized we are in the last inning of a great debt cycle. The previous great debt cycle was the Great Depression of 1929.

There are certain inevitabilities in life and soon we will face extraordinary events.

The rise of technology disruption, bringing a deflationary economy. The fall of a monetary system, getting a new currency system. The rise of a superpower, China, and the weakening of the USA.

Dalio says that 9 out of 16 great debt cycles end up in wars, and that's something the world doesn't want to happen anymore. Yet, China is moving faster in the CBDCs- they want to take advantage.

Of course, the USA is too powerful to let this opportunity go away. They will want to keep supremacy as the dollar continues to weaken.

We all must be aware of what central banks and governments are preparing for our future. We also have to prevent and know how to expect. To be winners, in these times of significant changes, is a patience exercise.

As the Fed keeps printing money, assets will keep rising. You should take the opportunity to earn as much as possible, but always with the prospect of reinvesting in hard assets: real estate, gold, or Bitcoin.

These are going to be the havens for an uncertain future.

I'm not a financial adviser. It's my opinion, but it's also the opinion of those who manage much wealth, like Paul Tudor Jones, Ray Dalio, Warren Buffett, Howard Marks, or Stanley Druckenmiller.

I hope you find this piece a helpful one. Be safe.

THE FEDERAL RESERVE'S TERRIFYING DEAD END

Who's going to be the number one with China's astronomical rise.

If you've been analyzing the dollar's macroeconomic structure and the United States monetary system, you get the feeling that we're getting to the end of something that no one knows what it is.

The dollar has fifty years as the main reserve currency in the world. A half-century may seem to be the magic number, but most analysts predict we're getting to the end of the dollar.

And one of these people is Ray Dalio. One of his phrases did bother me.

For example, if you don't understand how the Roaring '20s led to a debt bubble and a significant wealth gap, and how the bursting of that debt bubble led to the 1930–33 depression, and how the depression and wealth gap led to conflicts over wealth all around the world, you can't understand the forces that led to Franklin D. Roosevelt being elected president. You also wouldn't understand why, soon after his inauguration in 1933, he announced a new plan in which the central government and the Federal Reserve would together provide a lot of money and credit, a change that was similar to things happening in other countries at the same time and similar to what is happening now. Ray Dalio on LinkedIn

Accordingly to the Congress Budget Office, the U.S. federal budget deficit is projected to be $2.3 trillion in fiscal 2021. This number doesn't include the $1.9 trillion already issued. Last year was $3.13 trillion.

To put these numbers in perspective, the financial crisis of 2008 forced the Fed to inject money into the banking system to save it from collapse. It was called the TARP — Troubled Asset Relief Program. To save banks, the Fed printed about $700 billion.

At that time, it was a ton of money. People were astonished about the amount of debt the Fed was putting into the system. However, today you compare these numbers, and it seems crumbs.

The problem is that the markets are recovering, but the real economy isn't. So, the United States of America will keep needing more and more stimulus.

The Keynesian Multiplier is a theory that states that the economy will flourish the more governments spend. Yet, if the governments surpass 90% of their debt-to-GDP, they're in trouble from a macroeconomic perspective.

What usually happens is that after you surpass 90% of the debt-toGDP, the more you spend, the less your multiplier is your friend. Meaning, less and less growth will happen as the spending rises. And that's what's happening to the USA. The American debt-to-GDP is around 130% right now.

So, how are things going to work from now on?

———————— *NF* ————————

Promises Make Debt, and Debt Makes Promises

From a macroeconomic perspective, the most critical question you should make is:

How are we going to pay our debt?

First, you need to understand whom they borrow money from because everything is a supply and demand issue.

If a country has good credit, the same government will pay a lower rate. If a country has bad credit, it will pay a higher rate, and fewer institutions are interested in funding that same country.

Debt equals bonds.

A bond is simply a loan taken out by a company. Instead of going to a bank, the company gets the money from investors who buy its bonds.- Investopedia.com

Since August of last year, the 10-year Treasury yield has doubled. Meaning, the USA is paying two times the yield they did a couple of months ago. And that's a red flag. This red flag tells us the confidence from sovereign countries and institutions to lending money to the USA is decreasing.

If nobody is interested in funding the USA, they have to fund themselves. That's what they've been doing by buying their debt. Thus, they are abusing their position as dominators of the world's most powerful currency- the US dollar.

It's like a snake eating its own tail.

You Can't Have a Million-Dollar Dream With a MinimumWage Work Ethic

Everything is expensive. The houses are costly; the stock markets are expensive, and the food price is rising. Why?

Everything is costly because the dollar is losing value.

The US dollar is the reserve currency of the world. Approximately 60% of the world's transactions are executed in US dollars. Sovereign countries protect themselves by buying US treasury bonds.

Having external institutions and countries to pressure government bonds to rise in interest, the Fed has two options:

1) Prop Up Bonds

To control the rise of interest rates, the Fed can buy bonds. The Federal Reserve will manage the yield curve control by buying bonds to hit a specific rate target.

The problem with this strategy is that it will kill the currency. It will kill the dollar.

2) Strengthen the US Dollar

The United States of America will want to keep its reserve status as the number one reserve currency globally. So, they'll increase their economy with stimulus and state investments to attract foreign capital, lower imports, and rising exports.

Conclusion

The US government will determine one of these two options. I firmly believe that the Fed will prop up the bond market.

If the bond market blows up, it results in a systemic crisis, and the entire world economy would collapse. And the USA doesn't want that to happen because it would expose the reserve status, yet they don't want to lose control.

The US treasuries are the free risk most senior level of debt. It's the pillar of the entire debt system. If the bond market implodes, the whole system collapses.

The dollar being the senior reserve asset, it's also the collateral of all the derivatives markets. A derivative is a financial security with a value that is reliant upon or derived from, an underlying asset or group of assets — a benchmark.

The derivative market is where the most prominent institutions and banks speculate. On one side of the coin, it's a risky market, and betting it's something that public opinion does not appreciate. But on the other side, the market flows with capital that helps many companies thrive and be capitalized to improve and develop.

Bank of International Settlements, the central bank of all the central banks, estimates that the derivatives market is about $600 trillion.

Can you imagine a $600 trillion market instantaneously collapsing?

---------------------------- *nf* ----------------------------

Final Thought

The Great Reset initiative has a set of dimensions to build a new social contract that honors the dignity of every human being.- World Economic Forum

Ironically, the World Economic Forum talks about a great reset, pointing out the Covid-19 as its main trigger. Yet, the debt problem came much earlier. And unfortunately, the political system makes every burden to be transferred to the next guy coming into power.

A fears negotiation to reset the system, and so, to renegotiate the debt is a scary scenario.

Yet, the WEF did take the first step by making public the need to start reflecting about a plan b before everything collapses.

We don't know what the future will hold, but we are smart enough to protect ourselves from the Great Tsunami.

One way to do that, it's by not playing the game. I know people that sold every asset correlated to the market. So, they have lowered their exposure to the markets.

You can also buy real hard assets, like gold, silver, real estate, or Bitcoin.

Another way to protect yourself from playing the game is through emerging markets. Ray Dalio often gives that kind of advice to protect investors from the dollar itself.

But I'm a real fan of deep thinking and deep learning.

It's important to know what is going on. And act accordingly through our good sense and risk profile.

I hope you'll be on the right side of the storm, protected from the gigantic waves. And more importantly, ensuring the safety of your family and friends.

It's going to be an exciting year to follow.

PART II: THE WORLD IS CHANGING

THE GAMIFICATION OF THE ENTIRE ECONOMY: HOW THE NEW WORLD IS BEING DESIGNED

Enabled by crypto, digitally native economies are quickly emerging.

Have you ever watched the movie Ready Player One by Steven Spielberg?

Prepare yourself because this article will talk about strange concepts, virtual themes, digital ideas, and basically, how the future is being designed.

I'm 45 years old and I spend half of my life playing a strategy soccer game called Football Manager. Yet the digital world belongs to GenZ and there are currently 68 million citizens between 6 and 24 years old in the United States alone.

This generation of young kids is the first one born into a full digital era. We can add here also GenY, that are currently between 25 and 29 years old. GenY and GenZ are the builders of new digital infrastructures like Ethereum, Cardano, or Polkadots.

These two generations live in The Metaverse universe.

The Metaverse: a persistent, live digital universe that affords individuals a sense of agency, social presence, and shared spatial awareness, along with the ability to participate in an extensive virtual economy with profound societal impact.- Piers Kicks

This idea emerged in the late 80s and early 90s with Neal Stephenson and William Gibson, two American authors that created the term speculative fiction in a kind of cyberpunk style that produced the idea of evolving into a shared and persistently virtual world.

This is where the Ready Player One world emerges. Like the Steven Spielberg movie, millions or even billions of people will interact with each other in a new exceptional virtual environment.

Every single industry is being disrupted by the digital world, with Artificial Intelligence having a considerable influence in the robust implementation of algorithms and the cryptographic empowerment of the Web 3.0. The blockchain community and the gamification of the entire economy are things that will most certainly happen soon.

But, how does gamification work? What will be the implications in our daily routines? Will the gamification of the entire economy create individual sovereignty, justice, and equalitarian opportunities?

--------------------- *nF* ---------------------

Gamification can lead to high levels of learner engagement and motivation.

I recently wrote an article about Synthesis. A unique school created in Elon Musk's SpaceX facilities was built out of the concept of the gamification of education.

Synthesis wants their students to be the best collaborative problemsolvers out there. Synthesis recipe for learning is composed of:

- Simulation mechanisms
- Simulation concepts
- Mental models
- Team reflection
- Simulation analysis
- Personal reflection

Synthesis mixed the right ingredients to create the best circumstances for teaching and learning. Facilitators (teachers) only interfere in teamwork activities to prompt moments (they call them CLICKS) that set the suitable events for specific problems.

You can see here how Synthesis is gamifying the learning processes into a disruptive new school system.

A venture capital company called Duolingo is also disrupting the EdTech market. They created a free app that is simple to use and gamified adaptive language teaching for smartphones and web browsers.

Duolingo is an online language-learning app. It's pervasively and thoughtfully gamified: points, levels, achievements, bonuses for "streaks," visual progression indicators, even a virtual currency with various ways to spend it. The well-integrated gamification is a major differentiator for Duolingo, which happens to be the most successful tool of its kind. With over 60 million registered users, it teaches languages to more people than the entire US public school system.- Kevin Werbach, Associate Professor of Legal Studies and Business Ethics, Wharton School at University of Pennsylvania

———————————— *nF* ————————————

The story of gamification isn't fun and games by any means. It's serious.

When used carefully and thoughtfully, gamification produces great outcomes for users, in ways that are hard to replicate through other methods.- Kevin Werbach and Dan Hunter

Piers Kicks defined Metaverse as the complete digitization of everything. The gamification of everything will also be a strong possibility because the gaming incentives involve understanding psychology, design principles, and leveraging data. It actually taps into what makes us human.

Werbach and Hunter explain how games can be a valuable tool to address severe pursuits like marketing, productivity enhancement, education, innovation, customer engagement, human resources, and sustainability.- Kevin Werbach and Dan Hunter

As we spend more time in the digital world, we end up creating value, exchanging value, and earning some sort of crypto assets that we can transfer at the speed of light in the web 3.0 lightning network- Ethereum and other blockchains are constantly being created.

These platforms don't necessarily have to exist in the physical world because as time goes by, physical and digital value will be the same.

And in a Ready Player Go style, the gamification of the entire digital world will incentivize more and more people to drop from the physical world into the digital one.

For example, this week, the Bridgewater CFO, Dalby Leaving, shifted away from one of the bigger hedge funds to join the Bitcoin financial services firm NYDIG.

Dalby will be the organization's CFO, NYDIG said in a statement Friday. It offers customers Bitcoin custody, execution, and financing and is a subsidiary of $10 billion alternative asset manager Stone Ridge. NYDIG recently raised more than $300 million from strategic partners, including Massachusetts Mutual Life Insurance Co. and Liberty Mutual.- bloomberg.com

In a recent announcement, NYDIG made public that Bitcoin is coming to hundreds of US banks this year. So it's not just human resources coming from the physical to the digital world- it's much more than that.

These shifters are the ones that are making significant structural changes within the financial system.

NYDIG plans on other services, including debit card rewards paid in bitcoin and a new type of bank account called Federal Deposit Insurance Corporation (FDIC) insured but pays interest in bitcoin.- Hugh Son from cnbc.com

Let your intuition lead the way.

In a gamified world, the new financial structure is used by generations that grew up playing games and that somehow also built their tokens and communities in an intuitive way.

Gamification has long been applied to learning and marketing. Just think of how the military has embedded gaming techniques into its flight simulators. Today, businesses and marketers — especially in the consumer space — regularly employ gaming techniques.

Gaming techniques, such as leader boards, simulations, challenges, "top scorers," and the like, are natural extensions of performancebased work.

Additionally, Reward & Recognition professionals are probably best positioned to both use and move this vital concept forward.- theirf.org

The power of a gamified financial world, with all due concerns in terms of regulation, proof-of-work, and proof-of-stack, is that millions or even billions of people could gain access to your inventory or your avatar in a specific token or community you create.

The powerful networking effect this tokenization will bring to the financial world, combined with the good incentives of a gamified environment, can create a massively colossal boom of new businesses and new digital economies, where every citizen in the world with a phone or digital device can participate.

--------------------------------- *nF* ---------------------------------

Final Thoughts

The Exponential Age is coming.

Yet western societies have a fundamental structural problem: the robots are coming to take our jobs. Governments will have a hard time fighting unemployment because of the disruptive innovation that is replacing human work opportunities.

For example, look at your phone and ask yourself how many apps you have. Most of them are free to use. Now ask yourself how many jobs disappeared due to those apps. You probably have your bank on your phone, right? You probably take one thousand photos and put them in the cloud, right?

For that to happen, many jobs had to disappear.

Any function that is predictable and routine will be a target for improving efficiency through automation. This automation will aggressively replace the work of highly rewarded professionals.

However, it will not be all bad. Remember, technology is made by humans, and innovation has never harmed the development of humanity- quite the contrary.

The truth is that many jobs will disappear, but new jobs will be created in an economy that will change substantially in the coming decades.

A smaller range of people will probably be needed to work in specialized productive roles, as robots will do the rest. But new opportunities will be created, well paid, and valued by the community.

In an economy that is gamified but highly robotized and digitized, modern societies will be more sensitive to the protection of nature and natural resources and the care of an increasingly aging society.

We will more often be looking at the stars and sending rockets to other planets. We will demand the extinction of hunger and injustice, creating communities and tokens that will have the power to reach all corners of the globe in a philanthropic torrent never seen before.

Like with any other technological disruption, the economy is being redesigned by those who are willing to change. The Baby Boomers are getting old; GenZ and GenY are those who are in charge now.

These young kids like Piers Kicks and Jack Mallers are very bright, intelligent, and knowledgeable young creators.

Combining GenZ and GenY youth and irreverence with the experience of Millennials and Baby Boomers, a new gamified economy is emerging.

We all need to be open-minded and embrace the new economic design that will bring individual sovereignty and abundance globally.

HOW CAN YOU TAKE ADVANTAGE OF THE THIRD INDUSTRIAL REVOLUTION

Anticipating what will come, makes you the smartest person in town.

Baby boomers and older generations have been living in a vertical political system for centuries.

However, the Millennials to GenZ grew up in the Internet generation. They grew up thinking that power has to do with the network they're engaged in. So for them, power is not vertical; it's lateral.

For younger generations, power is being meshed network after network where they benefit each other, in an open-source philosophy.

These concepts are hard to comprehend for older generations because they don't have that notion of power.

Yet, the power of communities is arising; there's no way out. **The Internet of Things** is here to stay and evolve into the next boom, the next renascence of the modern era.

The beauty of living in a renaissance moment is that we can retrieve what we lost the last time around. Just as medieval Europeans retrieved the ancient Greek conception of the individual, we can retrieve the medieval and ancient understandings of the collective. We can retrieve the approaches, behaviors, and institutions that promote our social coherence.- Douglas Rushkoff in We Went From Tribal to Individual. Something Else Must Come Next.

But what is The Internet of Things, and how will it impact our lives and change our habits?

———————————— *nF* ————————————

Life is the art of drawing without an eraser.

Our scientists today say that we're in the sixth extinction event of life on Earth. Yet, it doesn't appear in the newspaper's headlines.

This is a dramatic story about the human race, and nobody seems to care.

There have been five major extinction events over the last 450 million years. And each time the chemistry of our planet changed dramatically, passing the turning point, it turned into a massive die out.

After the massive die out, it takes up to 10 million years to get new life back on Earth.

I know everybody hopes for us to go to Mars and beyond, but are we really able to mess up our fabulous planet? Are we going to mess up our entire species because we weren't smart enough to realize we're playing with fire?

Scientists say that we could lose over half the species of life that inhabit the blue planet in the next seven decades.

We're all messing up big!

We, human beings, are the younger species on Earth. We've just been here about 200,000 years. **But there's no guarantee we're going to make it.**

The ocean currents are being changed with ice freshwater melts in Greenland and the Arctic. As a result, massive storms have been more frequent, and a few decades from now, they will be massively catastrophic.

Do we want this future for our kids and grandchildren?

We need a new economic model for our future, and we need it to be quick and global. And it has to move quickly in the developing countries as in the industrialized nations.

If we want to escape this dangerous extinction, we must drastically change our worldwide plan to deploy that terrible vision of human being's extinction.

We have to be off carbon in four decades everywhere. And this is not a political issue; it's a survival one. So, in this matter, there is no China or UK, there is no European Union of the USA. There's one single beautiful blue planet to take care of.

How can we project a plan of this magnitude?

As Jeremy Rifkin mentioned:

We need to step back and reflect on how the great economic paradigm shifts in history occur. (…) There have been at least seven major economic paradigm shifts in history, and they are very interesting anthropologically because they share a common denominator. And that is at a certain moment of time three technologies emerge and converge to create what we call in engineering a general-purpose technology platform.

What are those three technologies?

First, new communication technologies that turn our economy more efficient. In the first industrial revolution, in the 19th century, the British started with communication by inventing the steam-powered printing. Steam-powered printing was a giant leap forward, allowing the population to have quick fresh information.

Second, new sources of energy to more efficiently power our economic activities. For example, in the second industrial revolution, in the 20th century, the Americans invented the centralized electricity grid, which allows the telephone, another invention, to absolutely revolutionized entire industries boosted with cheap Texas oil.

And third, new forms of mobility and logistics allow us to move our daily economic activities more efficiently. In the 21st century, the self-driving cars will radically transform cities' landscapes, daily routines, structural jobs, everything.

When communication revolutions join with new energy sources and new modes of transportation, it radically changes our way of life- it actually even changes our consciousness and governance.

———————————— *nF* ————————————

Can we reach biosphere consciousness and global empathy in time to avert planetary collapse?

In the 24 hours since this time yesterday, over 200,000 acres of rainforest have been destroyed in our world. Fully 13 million tons of toxic chemicals have been released into our environment. Over 45,000 people have died of starvation, 38,000 of them children. And more than 130 plant or animal species have been driven to extinction by the actions of humans. (The last time there was such a rapid loss of species was when the dinosaurs vanished.) And all this just yesterday.- In " The last hours of ancient sunlight " by Thom Hartmann

If we could jump into the future, future generations would identify the Bronze Age, the Iron Age, and the Oil Age. This last one would be characterized as an era where the entire global population went into hysterical exploitation of natural resources and almost brew up the whole ecosystem.

It's all about fossil fuels.

Even our fertilizers, pesticides, or pharmaceuticals are made out of fossil fuels.

Before the 2008 Great Recession, the barrel of oil touched the $147, and then, the entire economy collapsed. When the price of a barrel goes above $95, the cost of commodities goes up, and consumption drops dramatically.

Everything is dependent on fossil fuels.

This is a convulsion of growth-shutdown, growth-shutdown, growthshutdown.- Jeremy Rifkin

When some other countries out of the OPEC (The Organization of the Petroleum Exporting Countries) tried to get out of the oil dependence, searching for alternative forms of producing energy, the OPEC countries started to flood the world with an oil price point around $30.

What happened to companies that started producing shale gas in the US and tar sands in Canada? OPEC wiped them out in a year and a half. Bankruptcies all around the US and Canada and a potentially new renewable industry suddenly disappeared.

After the bankruptcy process ends, the price of the barrel starts to go up again. Yet, where the oil production exists, failed states also exist. And we live in this strange global dynamical spiral — an unstable world for the next decades.

When Germany, one of the most efficient productive countries in the world dependent on oil infrastructures, post-industrial revolution communication infrastructures, and mobility and logistic groundwork from three decades ago, what have we been missing?

Economics is governed by the same laws that govern the universe, the solar system, and the biosphere on Earth. Not Newton's law that made us humans only account for 14% of the productivity.

"For every action, there's an equal and opposite reaction" made modern economists use it for the supply and demand premise- for every action of the supply side, there's an equal and opposite reaction on the demand side.

However, we've been modeling the entire economy under a false premise.

The planet Earth has plenty of energy coming from the Sun for billions of years. But we don't have more different matter coming down here in terms of fixed matter on our planet.

So, we extract energy from nature, and through our value chains, we store it, ship it, produce goods and services from it, consume it, and recycle some of it back to nature.

At every step of the conversion, we lose some energy in the process. In economics, it's called "aggregate efficiency."

Aggregate efficiency is the ratio of the potential work to the actual valuable work that gets embedded into a product or service.

Imagine a lioness chasing an antelope and kills him. Then, only 10 to 20% of the energy comes from the antelope into the lioness. That energy transfer is called aggregate efficiency.

The US started the second industrial revolution at the beginning of the 20th century with 3% aggregate efficiency. By 1990, the US got up to about 14% aggregate efficiency.

Germany reached 18.5% aggregate efficiency in the 2000s, and the world's record comes from Japan with 20% aggregate efficiency in the 1990s.

If the infrastructures are yet from the 20th-century industrial revolution in these ultra-efficient countries, we're trying to operate the infinite game with a finite mindset. Meaning, we want to take steps into a new revolution, but we're still fighting to survive with the old infrastructures.

――――――――――― *nf* ―――――――――――

Knowledge is the share experience you have as a social being.

Recent economists that happen to study physics added a third factor to productivity:

Better machines, better workers, aggregate efficiency.

Why do you think Elon Musk, a rocket scientist, vertically integrated these three factors in his business plan for SpaceX and Tesla?

A new conversion to communication, energy, and transportation will create the third industrial revolution.

Actually, in Germany, the Chancellor Angela Merkel already started it. President Biden has a 6 trillion dollar check from the Federal Reserve also to try to catch up.

With its Silk Road Economic Belt, China will improve multimodal transport connectivity on multilateral trade and economic growth in countries and regions across Europe, Africa, and Asia, in a 4 trilliondollar investment. It's running fast to the third industrial revolution.

The Internet of Things will be the base of the internet of communications, the internet of energy, and the internet of transportations. It will connect everything to everyone.

Millions and millions of sensors in the agriculture industry, in factories, in smart homes, in logistic pipelines, in self-driving cars, in warehouses, and in intelligent roads are sending data. All of them are collecting data into these three internet platforms, communication, energy, and transportation, to manage power and move economic life.

We're building a nervous system that connects everything to everyone that's going to allow everyone on this planet, at a meager cost, to engage with each other on a global Internet of Things.

The population on Earth will be able to connect with each other very efficiently, in a vertically integrated grid, without the middleman that kept us away from each other.

This is the revolution.

This third industrial revolution is not centralized but globally distributed. It will be collaborative, open, and transparent. It will use smart contracts to disrupt the middleman and get ultra-efficient.

Millennials and GenZ will enter into a shared network, built under the premises of communities or tokens that will build low-energy solutions to solve old post-industrial revolution constraints in a highly efficient way.

A vast expansion of entrepreneurialism will rise into global neutral networks in a Snowden's fashionable way.

Every citizen will share their data and pick up some of them to mine it, giving input into the ecosystem, and everything will exponentially grow in an open-source network.

In billions of new value chains, everyone can create new apps, code, or algorithms and dramatically increase the aggregate efficiency of a token, a community, a project, or a company.

Final Thoughts

Entire industries have been disrupted in the 17 years since Napster.

The music industry has shrunk. The television audiences have shrunk since Youtubers created a new industry. Facebook has disrupted our social network, Tesla has disrupted the auto industry, and Amazon has disrupted the retail sector.

In 1978, the price of the kilowatt/hour on solar was $78. Today, power and utility companies are quietly buying long-term contracts for solar and wind in Europe and the US for 4 cents per kilowatt/hour.

It's game over for the oil industry.

What is happening in the cryptocurrency industry? The Bitcoin network and the blockchain are disrupting the entire financial system. As a result, a new economic system arises, decentralized, transparent, and at zero margin call.

Thousands of new enterprises have been created new projects under completely opposite premises. They are making the networks, the connectivity, the platforms, and the blockchains.

The zero-margin call and sharing society are gaining terrain, transforming the old analog ecosystems into new ones. Margin call societies are the new economic structure built under a deflationary ecosystem. Meaning, new projects are being designed to be efficient, at zero cost margin, creating new bases for new creations, sectors, or industries in endless cycles.

There are some doubts about the robotization of the entire industry- if it will eliminate job opportunities or create new ones.

However, for the next two decades, things will change dramatically and quickly, like any other technological disruption.

Economic attributes like digital thinking, mechanical and electronic competencies, and biological skills will be powerful tools to dominate this new economy.

Also, human attributes like kindness, competence, communication skills, artistic capabilities, vision, courage, and organized capacities will be human characteristics that will outstand in a robotized economy.

You must be open-minded in the following decades to thrive through this new technological disruptive era.

Knowledge will be the best asset to shift our mindsets into this new world.

YOU HAVE TO UNDERSTAND THE 'FOURTH TURNING' TO TAKE ADVANTAGE OF YOUR FINANCIAL FUTURE

Anticipating what will come, makes you the smartest person in town.

Dramatic events have marked the rhythm of economic and cultural cycles for centuries.

Whoever has the opportunity to understand these cycles will always have the advantage of identifying the signs, anticipating the events, and taking all kinds of hedges.

Understanding the 'fourth turning' is a crucial exercise, even more so today, when we are approaching the last half of the last cycle.

Something dramatic happens at the end of the fourth cycle, where social motivations, political and cultural structures, and individualism are called into question, reformulated, and a new order is born from the ashes.

You can have these sources for free and anticipate what opportunities the near future will bring.

———————————— *NF* ————————————

I have resolved to live, not just endure, each season of my life.

Every two decades, people change how they feel about themselves, the culture, the nation, and the future.

Like the seasons of the year, the 'fourth turning' comes in cycles of four. Each cycle takes the time of a human being, about 80 to 100 years. The ancients call it "the saeculum."

Jim Rohn wrote one of the books that most influenced me, called "Seasons of Life," where he presented a philosophical glimpse into the common threads interwoven among the laws of nature and humankind. Jim said simple things like this:

We sometimes can accumulate a mixture of the people and environments of life which, if not altered in some way, will assure that our future will be just about like our past.

Understanding the seasons of life is an effort to try to anticipate what comes next to summer. We all have winter seasons in our lives. But do we usually anticipate them?

The ancients had to do that exercise to survive. Yet, today, we are so comfortable thinking things are in control that we underestimate the importance of the winter. However, every single year, there it comes.

——————————— *NF* ———————————

First turning- the HIGH cycle.

The last HIGH cycle took place after the World War II, from the mid1940s to the 1960s.

An era where institutions were strong, and individualism was weak.

Society was confident about where it wanted to go collectively; the families had a strong bond, citizens reinforced institutions, an innocent cultural movement arrived, and had maximum community spirit.

It started in 1946 and ended in 1963 with the assassination of J.F.Kennedy.

Second turning- the AWAKENING cycle.

The last AWAKENING cycle was from the 1960s to the 1980s. People attacked institutions in the name of personal and spiritual autonomy. Just when the society is making its high level of public progress, people suddenly were tired of social discipline and wanted to recapture authenticity.

Third turning- the UNRAVELING cycle.

The last UNRAVELING cycle took place from the early 1980s to 2008.

Institutions were weak and untrusted, while individualism was strong and blooming. Unravelings follow the awakenings that follow a society of enjoyment. Highs were against the militarization of geopolitical strategies.

This cycle ended with maximum individualism and eroded institutions.

Fourth turning- the CRISIS cycle.

The next CRISIS cycle is where we are right now. From 2008 to 2030, the fourth cycle will turn institutions down and rebuild a new order from the ground up, always responding to a preserved threat to the nation's very survival. You had a recent episode with the invasion of the Capitol in Washington.

Civic authority revives, cultural expression finds a community purpose and people begging to locate themselves as members of a larger group.

In every instance, the fourth turning will eventually become new founding moments in America and the western world's history, refreshing and refining national identities.

New social structures will gravitate to new solid rising communities.

———————————— *NF* ————————————

Final Thoughts

There is a symbiotic relationship between historical events and the shape of different generations.

In our paradigm, the western world entered the fourth cycle, the CRISIS cycle. It started in 2008 with the Great Depression, where the entire population highly discredited institutions, commercial banks, and central banks. You have several great movies made after 2008 about the loss of morality from those who rule and were related to that crisis.

The fourth cycle will end in 2030, so we're halfway there. However, adding to all this, we are going through an era of profound technological disruption.

Nothing happens by chance. After the disruption of our social network (Facebook), the distribution industry (Amazon), the electronics industry (Apple), and the automotive industry (Tesla), only the financial sector is missing.

Yet, curiously, an anonymous citizen shared a 9-page white paper on the web, right after the 2008 crisis, and 12 years later, we are witnessing the total disruption of the financial world with Bitcoin and the blockchain.

Renewed institutions will need much flexibility to embrace this unstoppable Bitcoin tsunami.

In the USA, several states are already ahead and embraced it. The European Union is rapidly taking time to understand how they can take advantage of this technology. Even China and India, who initially forbidden its use, assume that it's impossible to stop the movement.

The future politicians and public infrastructures will be shaped by the values and aspirations of the rising millennials.

It started with a catalyst, the 2008 Great Recession, where people understood the fragilities of the system and started to redesign a new path. Millennials saw that they were not going to have the same privileges as their parents. So, they produced new ways of wealth creation.

Soon we'll have a regenerative event, where some politicians or some movements will find increase trust to redesign institutions. We'll wait and see who there is. But someone will appear to break the ice and give the world a new perspective to moralize institutions and rebuild trust.

A crisis will happen, and it will be radical or controlled. This event will occur when the ice breaks. When the pressure rises and the will of civic movements pressure institutions for change, radical decisions will happen, and the crisis turns into a new world.

With the resolution happening after the crisis, new treaties will be signed, negotiations are made, and the civil movements that were boiling suddenly solidify and take on a new life, with new rules and new ambitions.

Be sufficiently open-minded to do the right questions, to deeply understand what is going on with the new infrastructures that are being created.

In the financial world, an all-new world is being created, embraced not only by states or countries but also by citizens worldwide.

In an era where robots will take most of our jobs and human attributes will be the new gold, the common sense will radically reshape economic value.

And the web 3.0, or now called the blockchain lightning network, is being used by millions of people, especially from developed countries, to find new opportunities they never had, to fight inequality, authoritarianism, and poverty.

The western world dashes into the end of the fourth turning.

It's up to us to be on the right side of the road. Perceive all the signals that have been sent to you. Study in-depth what is going on in the world, ask the right questions, and make better decisions.

If you anticipate what will come, money will be a natural consequence of your deep thinking.

THE FUTURE WILL BE DECENTRALIZED

How the blockchain will bring hope to 3 billion people around the world.

4 billion people live in a banked and documented world. Yet, the other 3 billion people are unbanked and undocumented.

Why does this matter?

As it tends to a more banked and documented world, things like life expectancy, wealth, or equal opportunities, also tend to increase.

On the other hand, in an unbanked and undocumented world, poverty, insecurity, and low life expectancy are unfortunate.

So, we live in this bifurcated world, where centralized systems benefit half of the world's population. And leave the other half on the brink of poverty, without any opportunities to thrive in life.

In the USA, a middle 30 year old Jack Nash went to university, got married, owns a house and a car, and has a bank account. But also, has borrowed money, has several insurance policies, and sends some money to his cousin in Kansas.

In Sudan, a 30 to 35 years old Hassan Alaydrus, we don't know his age for sure because there's no reliable documentation. So we don't know about the work he's been doing. Hassan lives in an unneeded land, uses a bicycle for transportation, and his criminal history is complicated to verify. He lives in a cash economy, his assets are uninsured, and he receives money from his brother from Egypt, but he pays 15% tax exchange.

Hassan makes his life work only on verbal agreements, and he doesn't have access to the internet.

This is the reality for almost 3 billion people worldwide.

So, let's see some differences between these two cases:

- Jack sends money to his cousin at a residual transaction rate. Hassan pays a 15% tax rate to have his brother's money back.

- Jack has reliable, low-cost access to credit. Even if Hassan had access to credit, the interest rates would be between 35–80% interest (CGAP est.).
- If a war breaks out in Hassan's country, how can he prove his property ownership when he returns? Hassan is basically off the grid. Jack, on the other hand, lives in a system where there are legal records of possession.

Peruvian economist Hernando de Soto estimates assets and properties lock 10 trillion dollars' worth of value in underdeveloped countries due to this lack of documentation.

Experts have found a direct correlation between a nation's wealth and an adequate property rights system. This is because real estate is a form of capital, and capital raises economic productivity and thus creates wealth.- Loup Brefort, Country Manager for Serbia, The World Bank

So, what's the solution? How can we fix this brutal inequality?

— *nF* —

The Blockchain is going to change everything more than the Internet has.

Three significant structures will dramatically influence the global financial system.

- Blockchains, decentralized transaction systems, and smart contracts.

Blockchains

Are a specific type of database that stores data in blocks. Those blocks are then chained together. And as they're filled with data, they're chained onto the previous block. That way makes the data chained together in chronological order. Blockchains are used in a decentralized way so that no single person or group has control. Blockchains are immutable, which means that the data entered is irreversible.

It's the perfect place to put property rights, credentials, identities, and agreements. The Blockchain is censor-free.

Decentralized transaction systems

Namecoin:

Namecoin's flagship use case is the censorship-resistant top-level domain, which is functionally similar to .com or .net domains but is independent of ICANN, the main governing body for domain names.- Wikipedia

The .com and .net solutions are data-based protocols, usually centralized in the USA.

Namecoin is a company that wants the decentralize everybody by creating a new DNA system for the Internet.

Blocksign:

This new company launched its electronic signature platform.

The service allows users to upload a document and put a legally binding signature stamp on it with the time and date. Users can then maintain private records of what has been signed and who signed it.- laninfotech.com

A new era for legal binding is emerging. With these blockchain signature stamps, a more reliable, cheap, and efficient way of agreements between two parts will transform entire industries.

Etherium:

Ethereum is a technology that lets you send cryptocurrency to anyone for a small fee. It also powers applications that everyone can use, and no one can take down.- etherium.org.

Vitalik Buterin is a Russian-Canadian programmer and writer who is best known as one of the co-founders of Ethereum.

A brilliant 19-year-old mind created a white paper that, in 42 days, raized 18 million dollars to develop this platform.

Ethereum is for more than payments. It's a marketplace of financial services, games, and apps that can't steal your data or censor you.

Smart Contracts

Smart contracts will create decentralized versions of currently centralized services. You have examples as Amazon or eBay. But also financial products as stocks, bonds, and ETFs will be decentralized.

Smart contracts can be made by tokenizing web services. It also brings all the internet services and products into the Blockchain using no third parties or intermediation but the code.

———————————— *nF* ————————————

Final Thought

Remember our friend Hassan Alaydrus from Sudan?

Blockchain solutions could bring him the ability to get credit, property ownership, low transfer cost transactions, and historic reputation.

Hassan would be enabled to build a censorship-resistant always accessible digital history. The entire Hassan's data that are in the blockchain are there forever, without the intermediation from his government.

With his digital history on the blockchain, new metrics can evolve in a Defi (decentralized finance) system. They can provide credit, reliable documentation, criminal history, and insurance policies. But also enable his brother to send him money from a foreign country for a nominal fee.

Micro-finance and micro-insurance will unlock small economies from their government's manipulations.

Only 20% of the Africa population has access to a banking account. But fortunately, two-third of Africans have access to a cell phone. So, many people from poor countries may have access to the Blockchain, and therefore, all their services and products.

The future will be decentralized. And that's all good news.

If the blockchain would only solve these micro-constraints of developed countries, it would have been worth it.

THE EXPONENTIAL AGE IS COMING: UNDERSTANDING IT WILL BE YOUR MOST VALUABLE FINANCIAL HEDGE

Everything is being sucked into this new financial world, and you've got not to be left behind.

I think we've entered The Exponential Age: an era where the digital and physical paths finally converge and everything is disrupted- for good.- Raoul Pal in realvision.com

Our brains are programmed to think linearly, and that's the main reason we have so much difficulty picturing the exponential growth concept.

However, we can grab the example of Kodak to understand more straightforwardly the difference between linear and exponential phenomenon.

Kodak created the first digital camera in 1975. Yet, the company quit developing such innovative creations because it didn't want to damage its monopoly in the photographic film business.

At that time, it was like inventing electricity, but then quit because you wouldn't want to interfere with the candle business.

Kodak was slowly eaten in the following decades, being delisted in 1999 from the DJIA index, being there more than 7 decades long.

We can hear many stories about Kodak, but the exponential nature of the digital camera technology and its network effects led to a massive increase in adoption from the mainstream.

The power of technology disruption is exponential.

That's why we're entering **The Exponential Age**, where we can see all sorts of disruptions in different industries, from retail, auto, energy, and social networks. These are sectors where the digitization is so vital that it sucks everything like a black hole.

Two of the most important questions to do right now are How much can a financial disruption interfere with our wellbeing as a global society? Is economic disruption going to give every single citizen different tools to thrive in a more equalitarian system?

————————————————— $\mathcal{NF}$ —————————————————

There can be an economy only where there is efficiency.

The pandemic was a massive event. Every government and the central bank had to intervene with vast amounts of money to save the economy and help the citizens.

With a liquidation phase never seen in history, there was hope in the vaccines to change the scary trajectory of the virus. And the hope phase came with the vaccination taking place, herd immunity, and the slow opening of the global economy.

However, something unusual happened as well. The real economies never picked up for a while. They stayed precisely as expected. Yet, the markets did the opposite. The year-on-year GDP will be negative, but the markets are soaring like a spaceship.

The hope of an open economy was replaced with frightening structural unemployment. In Florida, restaurants are closing again because they don't have people to work. Citizens that lost their jobs are at home on subsistence.

Many people in retail are never going back to jobs again. There is a fundamental structural problem coming up.

If things happen naturally, the insolvency phase should make BBB entities like giant corporations run out of cash. That would naturally occur in the households too. The same would happen in the small businesses.

Governments did what they had to do, with instant transfer payments in an MMT style, with fiscal and monetary policies to save citizens and companies.

Unfortunately, this kind of action was what Japan has been done over the years, which doesn't leave us in the least optimistic perspective about the future.

Don't get me wrong, it helped many people, but it probably just delayed the insolvency phase that is coming next.

Technically, many firms, many people, many businesses are insolvent, but they're being kept alive by central banks and governments.- Raoul Pal in realvision.com

As the economy settles down and restart working at full speed, we still have significant challenges ahead. Of course, governments and central banks have to do everything in their power to avoid an insolvency phase. They will try everything to prevent rates from going up because they'll not allow any chance to destroy the economic recovery.

To control rates, governments and central banks have one last tool called yield curve control. They will buy U.S. Treasuries and government-backed debt as necessary to keep yields below a certain level.

However, once they cross that line, it becomes more challenging to find their way back. Central banks will throw out all the stops against the crisis. But if the market has a different idea of where the neutral 10-year yield stands, things can turn nasty.

———————— *nf* ————————

The lesson from behavioral economics is that people only save if it's automatic.

With the creation of the future CBDCs (Central Bank Digital Currency), central banks will have the capability to monetize money.
There are some qualities on it because it's programmable money.

Central banks will create programmable money so we all can have different monetary policies or tax regimes.

That means behavioral economics will take place. Central banks will completely control our money, our savings, or our ability to spend. In fact, is precise because of CBDCs that we all need, in the future, a lifeboat, some sort of tool to protect us from total control.

And Bitcoin is, for now, the best choice of all.

Yet, there's another challenge for governments shortly because debts keep rising indefinitely all over the world. So, this means, theoretically, they are all bankrupt, but in this world of printing mania, the rules are different if central banks can print endless amounts of money, but one question remains.

How do they finance that endless debt?

They will finance it with taxation, inflation, and debasement of the currency.

Taxation is going up everywhere in the world — no doubt about it.

Inflation is something so hard to control that one day, some event will happen, some kind of black swan episode, and it can come sooner than we think.

Deficits are not going away, so prepare for more fiscal stimulus because the debasement of currencies will not be enough to control these vast debts.

With this said, it's difficult to be optimistic about the future when facing a severe technological disruption, the aging population and the baby boomers' retirements coming soon, and all the globalization phenomenon from the developed countries.

My biggest concern is not about the quantitative easing or even the yield curve control resilience to save the global economy. My biggest concern is the inequality gap that has been created.

This monetary policy is getting hold out the middle class because wages are being destroyed, and with that, millennials cannot afford to buy houses or access assets compared to those who are benefiting from this policy- the richest.

———————————————— _nF_ ————————————————

Bitcoin will do to banks what email did to the postal industry.

Bitcoin was created to serve the highly political intent, a free and uncensored network where all can participate with equal access.- Amir Taaki

Bitcoin can be the foundational stone of what we need to build a new financial system. The most important reason why is that we're completely destroying the system we're in.

With this system, nothing collapses as the Fed keeps printing 120 billion dollars every single month.

The strange thing about this policy is that these numbers don't show up in the bond market. The actual numbers appear in the less financial power citizens, who are forced to buy, over time, assets with their fewer dollars. And because of that, their savings structures are getting worse and worse.

Another financial system is being built with refined collateral- the Bitcoin.

What do I mean by that? Right now, strange as it may seem, the US Treasuries are the collateral for the all market. Yet, you can create more of that. It's not finite. So, it's a strange game to play when you have rules constantly changing.

With Bitcoin, a 21 million units' protocol, you can't create more of it. As a collateral tool, it's theoretically more unhandled.

Bitcoin is also a great store of value because of the limited supply and the robust network.

Whatever you believe in the old system or in the new one, the most trusted one will win.

———————————————— nt ————————————

The technical side of the Ethereum's efficacy is 100% an engineering exercise.

The present potential power of the Ethereum network is of its capability to swallow the entire financial system, which is something overwhelming.

But what is the Ethereum network, after all?

Ethereum is an open-source, blockchain-based, decentralized software platform used for its own cryptocurrency, ether. It enables Smart Contracts and Distributed Applications (ÐApps) to be built and run without any downtime, fraud, control, or interference from a third party. (…) One of the big projects around Ethereum is Microsoft's partnership with ConsenSys. — investopedia.com

Ethereum is a platform on which you can build, deploy, and use decentralized applications that don't have a home in a singular computer but are distributed through the entire network, meaning the Internet. Every developer has to verify each other, which makes the system with high levels of trustworthiness.

Having Microsoft building something on top of the Ethereum platform means things are already changing.

The best and more straightforward example I can remember is like thinking of Windows 15 years ago. Microsoft Windows was the platform that has enabled many companies to take advantage of tools to maximize their businesses.

Yet, the Ethereum is a 100% decentralized platform. Any developer can build, share, or use the platform to create new applications for all to see clearly and transparently.

——————————— 𝓃𝓕 ———————————

Final Thoughts

The behavior incentives for Bitcoin and Ethereum to thrive are outstanding. Because of that, people involved in these technological innovations are going to be the first beneficiaries.

The power of Bitcoin and Ethereum was a purely behavioral economics-driven model.

For example, in Facebook, behavioral economics by Metcalfe's law made you invite your sister, your uncle, your grandma, and everyone you know into a specific network. Yet, with all the business brought into the Facebook network, the only ones who get rich were the shareholders, not the users.

All the Silicon Valley models were basically the same as Facebook's.

With Bitcoin and Ethereum, a network was created and driven by behavior economics, but the big difference is that every participant gets rewarded by inviting outside people in.

The behavioral incentive from Bitcoin and Ethereum participants is extraordinary.

In a world dominated by big banks, the only way to dematerialize money would be with a decentralized system with a solid behavioral economic structure.

And here we are, with Bitcoin having a one trillion-dollar market cap and Ethereum above 400-billion-dollar market cap.

They are sucking all the energy, time, and network effects of the financial world.

With the debasement of Fiat currency at a 15% yearly pace since the 2008 Great Recession, it gets challenging to find ways of preserving wealth. That's why so many people are looking at Bitcoin as a trustworthy solution.

Ethereum will keep force big companies to build their structures upon it, and that will happen because more and more business owners see it as the future of the Internet and the global network access.

The Exponential Age is already around us, growing roots around all industries. May we be aware of it, trying to understand how it is evolving.

To have the early adoption advantage, we must keep digging into these concepts with an open mind, trying to find bridges between what we believe is inevitable and new systems growing around us.

Keep an open mind; it's the only way new things can get in.- Colleen Hoover

PART III: THE ROBOTIC SWITCH

ROBOTS WANT YOUR BLOODY JOB. HOW TO REFINE HUMAN SKILLS TO LEVERAGE YOUR FUTURE

Think as a human, not as a machine.

If you ask an employer what he looks for in an employee, the answer would be something like "faster, cheaper, and more productive." Robots have no flaws. They are limited to execute command orders.

If you were an employer, who would you assign the job to?

Some believe that automation will destroy the productive workforce. For the last decades, intensive specialized jobs have been switched to robots.

The second wave of automation and artificial intelligence will wipe out middle management jobs. Especially professionals in law and medicine.

The highest-paid professionals, who have so far benefited from technological disruption, will find resistance in the most advanced technologies.

Large databases, advanced algorithms, inexpensive sensors, and all kinds of robotics will converge to face middle management's lucrative jobs. Any function that is predictable and routine will be a target for improving efficiency through automation.- John Pugliano in The Robots are Coming: A Human's Survival Guide to Profiting in the Age of Automation

In fact, AI, deep learning, microchips, and robotics will only tend to speed up the process. Its impact will be felt more quickly in the coming decades.

We cannot predict the future, but as unique human beings, we can anticipate and adapt to a new world. It will be tough, but also our salvation. We're the ones who make the machines, and we do it for our benefit.

In fact, human characteristics are unique, and machines will never be able to reproduce emotions and feelings, like us.

Human attributes will make a powerful difference in the future. Our attributes will be exclusive assets.

Machines will simply work to provide us free time.

What about our job? Will robots take every job in the world?

———————————— ⁊⫟ ————————————

Almost everything will work again if you unplug it for a few minutes, including you.

Work will be almost free.

It's hard for us to accept it, but it's going to be a reality. Much automation will bring bad news for workers but good news for consumers. Ironically, they are the same person.

Work almost free it's a complex concept to understand. The same way information almost free was challenging to believe 20 years ago, but it happened.

The most valuable information was only accessible in the great metropolises and in the university centers. Before the internet, you had to pay good money for info. Right now, you google it.

Work almost free will have the same trajectory. Robots will substitute human labor. Artificial intelligence, high-precision robotic, and deep learning will search for top payment jobs like doctors and lawyers.

Even China will have hard times soon. The country was a gigantic factory for 20 years. Yet, one entire factory with two thousand lowwage workers will be swift by robots and 3D printings.

The USA, on the other hand, will enjoy abundant and cheap resources. Recent discoveries of low-cost natural gas will give Americans a unique opportunity to expand production and innovation. These resources will transform North America into a future gigantic lowcost production cluster.

Through natural gas and robotics, the USA will increase its financial and geopolitical supremacy.

The deflationary power of technology will give more freedom and quality time to those who embrace it. It's a radical paradigm shift, but it's inevitable.

If everything- not just phones or Internet companies but everything- is giving far more performance and at the same time falling in price, a family that makes $75,000 this year and struggles to make ends meet could make $70,000 next year, and the dollars would go further. And then, $60,000 a few years after that, and it would go further still, continuing to gain more for less with the natural deflationary trend in technology. That would allow us to step off the existing treadmill of chasing higher and higher prices, requiring ever-higher-paying jobs to keep up.

That may sound radical, but if the technology is deflationary, and we expect technology to continue its advance into more and more industries, it may not be radical at all. It may be the only sane thing to do.- Jeff Booth in The Price of Tomorrow.

If technology should be driving everything cheaper, why is life getting more expensive?

--- *nF* ---

Technology is the foundation of the empowerment economy.

Everyone using a cell phone can have access to the Blockchain technology. These tools will improve underdeveloped countries, helping them to find their true independence.

Technology and creativity are two powerful creations. Both will flip principles at times considered inviolable.

Disruptive technologies are eliminating the intermediaries. It will change the concept of money and work. Millennials and gen Z see money in the most creative way. They'll be responsible for a new economy based on human behavior and happiness.

The global economy will shift to a completely different motto. The world digitization will put the human soul in the center of everything. And it will be the scarce asset of all.

———————————— *nF* ————————————

Nothing endures but personal qualities.

Personal attributes will be the game-changer of the future. The new generations will be born under entirely different premises.

Imagine your grandson or granddaughter born in an era where work is defined as helping other people. They'll not need to build anything because robots are here to do it for them. They just have to pick their brain and create.

According to John Pugliano, there are four main attributes:

- Digital thinking: It's the extension of deep learning and artificial intelligence. It's in the realm of zeros and ones that this attribute will navigate. It will be the primary catalyst in the evolution from analog to digital.
- Mechanical skills: In an era of robots, a lot of mechanical knowledge will be needed. Many of us will have a personal robot at our home and in our personal lives. We only need skills like design, installation, maintenance, reprogramming, dismantling, and disposal.
- Electronic knowledge: It will be an ideal way to support mechanical skills. The electronics will be the robot's brain. There will be robots everywhere, dependent on energy systems to operate. Skills in the field of electricity and electronics will always be needed.
- Biological skills: For those interested in life sciences, the opportunities will be abundant. Dismantling old rudimentary facilities from the coal and oil era will be a challenge for generations. But as bionics improve, we'll need genetic engineers.

These will be the mainstream attributes of a highly technological society. Some industries will be dismantled, and others will be redesigned.

———————————— *nF* ————————————

To handle yourself, use your head. To handle others, use your heart.

In the future, your uniqueness will not be a burden. People will want to know your personal attributes. Those skills will be the absolute differentiator in your ability to bring value to the world.

Kindness

In a highly mechanical world, kindness will be one of the most valuable personal attributes. Human interaction will have a higher value. People will be often in the presence of robots most of the time. If you see a cell phone like a robot, at some point we're already there. Yet, it will have a more significant impact in the future.

Robots will decrease dramatically the cost of everything, but in certain situations, you'll prefer a kind person to be in front of you. And you'll pay for that.

Competence

Data, cloud storage, and social networks will be intolerant to incompetence. Mechanical work will be exclusively executed by robots. But ultra-specific tasks will require total human delivery, concentration, and efficiency.

You already see this kind of phenomenon today. For example, if you need to choose between a taxi driver and a Uber, you'll choose fast. You'll select the system that informs you who's the taxi-driver.
You'll choose a clean, fast, and digitized service.

Communication

In the new era, being a Tim Ferriss is not enough. You must interlayer the incredible communication ability of Ferriss with the computing language. Those who will manage, for example, biological skills, are the future technicians of communication.

Artistic

This attribute will stand out, as we'll live in a more sterile and mechanized world. Artistic expression will be the primary way to highlight our uniqueness. It will be challenging to live exclusively from art. Yet, evolving artistic skills with one main attribute will be powerful. Art mixed with mechanical skills or electronic knowledge could be a magical formula.

Bravery

In a highly efficient world, entrepreneurship will have more and more value in the market. Public jobs will be scarce, and your ability to build your own career will have more impact on your success. Society will create all the tools you need to be an easy ride. However, a courageous attitude will be required. Remember the conditions will change quickly as technology evolves.

nf

Final thought

We all create strong expectations regarding our personal and professional growth. We take courses, read inspiring articles, and listen to the most experienced experts.

However, no one prepares us for what has not yet been invented. Apart from Marty McFly and Doc Emmet Brown, no one has before predicted the future.

There are clues left from the most entrepreneurs and audacious ones.

Makes perfect sense to assume human attributes as the differentiator factor.

Self-improvement is not a static process. We have good clues on how to improve our kindness, competence, communication, artistic, and bravery skills.

Almost instinctively, after reading this article, you'll try to improve them every single day.

In fact, super-efficient robots will need your unique attributes to perform all the tasks for which they were programmed.

Right there, you'll have the proof of your uniqueness.

THE NOBLE POWER OF BEING SUPERIOR TO ROBOTS IS WITHIN EACH ONE OF US

Think like a human, not like a machine. Think like an entrepreneur, not like an employee. Think like an economizer, not a consumer.

Robots will take our jobs.

Are we prepared for it? Of course not.

Nobody is even noticing that the robots are taking our jobs, but the truth is that they are.

Nobody knows what the future holds, but I'm sure that the robots will significantly impact unemployment rates, and it will be painful.

The signs of stagnation in the global economy have been feeling for decades. To feel productive and avoid crashes, we need moneymaking machines (central banks) to replace our GDPs. And the next few decades are going to be the accumulation of mountains of debt.

Robots are here to stay, but also to help us in our daily routines.

Not all news is bad. While some people will be fired to be replaced by robots, others will be hired for their human attributes.

But after all, what will distinguish us in the future, and how can we anticipate this trend as early adapters?

———————————— NF ————————————

Man is a slow, sloppy, and brilliant thinker; the machine is fast, accurate, and stupid.

If you ask an employer what he or she looks for in an employee, the answer would be something like "faster, cheaper, and more productive."

Some believe that the robotization of the productive industry will have a disproportionately negative effect on the working class. But the reality is that sometimes we forget the resilience that human beings have and the capacity and creativity that we use to produce new needs out of thin air.

The effect of this technological disruption will be felt most strongly by the previously protected working class, such as middle management, legal professionals, but also in medicine.

Better-paid workers, who have so far benefited from the efficiency of the information age, will soon encounter an unprecedented technological wave with overwhelmingly more effective and cheaper capabilities. Therefore, competition between the two entities will not even be a case of discussion.

Nobody knows the pace of this disruptive technological era. We don't even know what technologies will thrive in high voltage in the following years. Probably the adoption will accelerate as societies adapt themselves to these new mainstreams.

———————————— *nf* ————————————

Wisdom consists of the anticipation of consequences.

Technology is made by humans. We create new things with our ingenuity and creativity. But everything we search enables our curiosity to find new tools to use and benefit from them.

Although we might think that robots will take our jobs, we often forget that we are the ultimate creators. And this willingness to do better and different made us, humans, what we are today.

Our uniqueness makes us use technology to overcome different layers of development. Look what is happening with the disruption of money? Suddenly, every government in the world is preparing to shift to crypto. Why?

Innovation makes us change. Sometimes we are so sheltered in our comfort zone that we fight against the change. But the reality is that, whether we like it or not, when innovations become mainstream, there's no way to stop them.

In this disruptive era, some pieces of advice should stay in the air so that we, humans, can begin to deeply think so that radical changes don't have to come so highly, but in a progressively wave of minor trades.

We have to shift our mindset because the world demands it. Hence, we must think like humans and not machines, like entrepreneurs, not employees, like economizers, not consumers, and like investors, not spectators.

Our human attributes will be enhanced to the point that they can become the difference between having a challenging job or staying at home receiving any type of Universal Basic Income (UBI).

The rarest of the good qualities in human beings is courage.

We, humans, are incredibly efficient adaptative animals.

From generation to generation, some jobs turn obsolete because innovation makes activities unnecessary. Yet, specific human attributes stay with workers. Meaning, in jobs that no longer exist, workers develop particular characteristics or attributes that make them qualified for another kind of future job.

For example, in the 60s, office workers have developed human attributes in typing, work organization, and communication. These attributes can perfectly fit into current or future jobs.

Remember, human attributes will increase their value over time as robotic systems rise into most industries.

The main human attributes will always have more importance when combined with others. For example, Elon Musk is simultaneously the CEO of Tesla, SpaceX, Neurolink, and The Boring Company.

Entrepreneurs are not necessarily outstanding at just one function. On the contrary, entrepreneurs who will stand out the most in the future will combine different human attributes, which will improve their perception of needs, vision for the future, and flexibility for change.

So, what kind of human attributes are we talking about?

— nF —

Main attributes.

1. Digital thinking

It's the extension of deep learning and artificial intelligence. It's in the realm of zeros and ones that this attribute will navigate. It will be the primary catalyst in the evolution from analog to digital.

2. Mechanical skills

In an era of robots, a lot of mechanical knowledge will be needed. Many of us will have a personal robot at our home and in our personal lives. We only need skills like design, installation, maintenance, reprogramming, dismantling, and disposal.

3. Electronic knowledge

It will be an ideal way to support mechanical skills. The electronics will be the robot's brain. There will be robots everywhere, dependent on energy systems to operate. Skills in the field of electricity and electronics will always be needed.

4. Biological skills

For those interested in life sciences, the opportunities will be abundant. Dismantling old rudimentary facilities from the coal and oil era will be a challenge for generations. But as bionics improve, we'll need genetic engineers.

— nF —

Plant seeds of happiness, hope, success, and love; it will all come back to you in abundance.

Technology brings abundance because it's deflationary. Today you can count the number of free services that apps on the phone can offer you. Initially, they weren't free, but the deflationary trend tends to be accessible as new innovations are created.

For services to be free, jobs are lost.

Yet, we are on a planet of opportunities. Don't believe it's the end of the world, because personally, I think it's just the beginning of an abundant era.

We will enter an era in which people will be able to choose between human interaction and robotic automation.

Human interaction will undoubtedly be more expensive, as the abundance created by robots will make everything ridiculously cheap or even free, except for services provided by humans.

There will be some types of services that we will insist on being provided by robots, but other services we will not work without the human presence.

For example, imagine you will get your driving license. Do you prefer to be met by a sulky secretary at the Institute for Mobility and Transport? Or do you prefer to go through an online platform in the comfort of your home?

Another example: you were the victim of a robbery. Do you prefer to fill out an accident form online or be attended by a helpful law enforcement officer?

In the future, the economy will be highly dichotomous. There will be very cheap products provided by robotic services, but human attributes such as kindness will be highly paid and scarce in the job market.

In the world of robotic precision, incompetence will not be tolerated. Whatever one's job function, the fundamental quality standard will be competent execution of the task. Feedback from data exploration, cloud computing, and social media will instantly assess the performance of all jobs.- John Pugliano in The Robots Are Coming

So, **competence** will be a helpful human attribute if you know you're an exemplary worker.

Another crucial human attribute that will clearly distinguish us from robots is the **ability to communicate**. In a world of robotic questionnaires, the presence of a communicative human being, with sensitivity to manage conflicts, present understandable solutions, and capture the attention of large communities, will be one of the secret weapons for the future.

Art transforms itself into a digital product, with the non-tangible tokens (NFTs) completely revolutionizing the intermediation of art.

Art will take biblical proportions in a devised world because the human factor that art has in humanity today is already incredibly high.

Can you imagine yourself in a world where the zeros and ones, the code, and the algorithms will be part of our day-to-day?

Get ready to discover your artistic streak, as the **artistic attribute** will be highly valued by the future market.

The world of finance is changing at a rapid pace. Those who can't manage risk are doomed to be poor. The system has been built for individuals to transform themselves into little entrepreneurs. And managing risk is one of the things every individual should do to avoid the rat race most of us are trapped in.

Those who have more **courage** to face risk and take action in a technological era will thrive.

Yet, the risk always has to be managed in a balanced way. Entrepreneurs pay high prices if they don't control other human attributes like greed, lust, or envy.

———————————————— nF ————————————————

Final Thoughts

Think like a human, not like a machine.

Those who try to fight against the powerful force of technology will fail. Those who try to be more efficient than a robot in repetitive tasks will fail.

Remember, human attributes are things intrinsic to every human being. We just have to empower them to gain an advantage in a highly competitive era ahead.

Algorithms will reduce simple human tasks to dust.

In your job, you probably have that kind of worker that always tries to innovate, and it's always searching for new technological solutions to solve daily problems. That's the guy you have to follow. He probably constantly searches for innovative ways to do his job. You should start to do the same.

The power of being superior to robots is within each one of us. Artificial intelligence and deep learning will compete with humans.

Yet, the battle will not be won physically but in our curiosity, ingenuity, courage, and kindness.

MONEY REVOLUTION IS KNOCKING AT YOUR DOOR: WHY YOU SHOULD BE AN EARLY ADOPTER

An astonishing startup found the perfect network to make the shift.

Blessed are the meek, for they will possess the earth.(Matthew 5:5)

How can the meek survive when technology disruption steals most jobs?

We want to believe life is going well, the economy is working smoothly until it doesn't. Housing prices are going to the roof, cars are getting pricy, the stock market is at all times high, and the party goes on.

On the other hand, tech devices, clothes, and services are getting cheaper (especially online).

If technology is causing a deflationary movement, why are certain things getting more and more expensive?

It seems we have two worlds colliding with each other, and they actually are. Why?

Robots will take most jobs, and technology disruptions will move into just about every industry, and we should be watching a deflationary environment with the cost of everything going down.

Governments will do everything to stop deflation and control inflation at 2 percent a year, so they can keep money printing to increase spending. It's much easier for politicians to manage a country with endless budgets.

So, central banks and governments fuel the economy with credit and debit to mask what is really happening underneath.

Meanwhile, to join the party, a new digital world is being born, full of financial innovation, within the blockchain, in a deflationary movement unparalleled in human history.

The next episodes may have dramatic scenes if politicians do not realize that deflation will bring abundance. The problem is that this abundance can only appear if they lose some control of their power. And there, by itself, is already a huge problem.

--------------------- $\mathcal{NF}$ ---------------------

Lightning makes no sound until it strikes.

Several silent revolutions have been taking place while technology innovation thrives worldwide. Entire new networks have been built under new premises, like Facebook, Amazon, Apple, or Tesla.

The social network was dematerialized, and retail, mobile devices, and automobiles also entered into technological revolutions. Yet, money, wish is the most important one, has been left behind.

Meanwhile, a new network surges to take control- the Bitcoin network.

It's crucial to make the distinction between Bitcoin the asset and Bitcoin the network.

Bitcoin the asset is volatile, like any new safe-haven financial entity, and it's hard to custody.

Bitcoin the network, when compared to the Visa or PayPal network, gives you identity out of the box, gives you payment specifications, and combined with the lightning network, gives you instant cash finality in real-time at no cost.

The Bitcoin lightning network is the most inclusive monetary network of all time. Why? Simple. Can a citizen of El Salvador or Venezuela use a Visa or Mastercard free of charge or without being subjected to such a violent exchange that it leaves them with no money to spend? No.

The Bitcoin lightning network works in El Salvador as well as in Chicago, Lisbon, or Sydney. That's why it's the most inclusive network.

So, what is the Bitcoin lightning network, after all?

The Bitcoin lightning network.

There is a big issue standing in the way of Bitcoin the asset, which is its scalability.

One example is Visa, which provides 4,000 transactions per second, and can scale to a maximum of 65,000 transactions per second.

On the other hand, Bitcoin can handle up to 7 transactions per second with the current block size of 1MB. This main blockchain isn't very scalable, but it doesn't have to be.

The blockchain community comes up with a new technique called the lightning network that solves the scalability issue.

Everyday transactions don't have to be stored on the main blockchain. Transactions can be stored in an off-chain system.

Let's make an example to simplify the lightning network.

Imagine that Martha is buying a cappuccino every day at Starbucks. Creating a transaction on the Bitcoin blockchain for a simple cappuccino is hard to do, and it's costly. Yet, with the lightning network, Martha can set up a payment channel with Starbucks. Both have to deposit a certain amount of Bitcoin in a multi-signature address.

Imagine Martha is depositing 0.05 BTC, and Starbucks deposit nothing. The multi-signature address is like a safe that can only be opened when both parties agree.

When the open channel is produced, the two parties can create a balance sheet that says how the funds on the address should be distributed. All this process is in the blockchain, so it's fully transparent.

Starbucks can see that the customer Martha deposited 0.05 BTC and by so, be rest assured that they will get their money once the channel closes.

Now, the cappuccino costs 0.001 BTC, and Martha has to change the balance sheet, subtracting the cost of the cappuccino from her balance and adds it to Starbucks.

When Martha and Starbucks sign the updated balance sheet with their private keys, each of them keeps a copy of it, and that's it.

Martha can keep ordering stuff from Starbucks as long as she has sufficient BTC on her balance sheet. Martha can do thousands of transactions, and the system is cheaper and quicker than the main blockchain. The payment channel can be closed at any time by Martha or Starbucks. They just have to take their BTC from that specific address and brought it again to the Bitcoin network. Miners will validate the signatures of the balance sheet and, if everything checks out, release the funds according to the balance sheet.

The lightning network can significantly reduce the traffic on the main blockchain, and it's safe because both parties have a signed copy of the balance sheet.

If Martha's mother wants to buy a tea at Starbucks, she doesn't have to create another payment channel. The lightning network has a highly efficient system. It looks for the quicker address and uses it with the two parties who agreed to play new transactions.

———————————————— ƞℱ ————————————————

How young engineer Jack Mallers designed the future of Strike.

Kjell Inge Røkke, a Norwegian billionaire, recently wrote to his shareholders a letter about Jack Mallers that says:

In the past months, I have met many new people. One of them was Jack Mallers of Strike. He's almost forty years younger than me. Experiencing his energy and enthusiasm was special. I felt old in his company but also very emboldened: I lost out on mobile communications. I didn't invest in Internet companies. It was only recently that I started to invest in and build software companies (and I love it!) When I realized how much brainpower goes into Bitcoin, I saw the future in the making.

Mallers' grandfather directed the Chicago board trade, and since a young age,

Jack has been surrounded by all kinds of conversations between his grandfather, his father, and his family about stocks, bonds, derivatives, and financial tools.

In an innovative disruptive era, Jack emerges as this fantastic entrepreneur, with an extreme notion about the markets, but better than that, ultimately appeared in the ecosystem of blockchain and Bitcoin.

So, to explain what Strike does, let me explain monetary networks.

Some of the most popular financial networks are the SWIFT, Visa, PayPal, Square, and Mastercard. As networks, what do all these known systems do? For example, Visa uses ACH (automated clearing house) plus the Visa network to move US dollars, implementing things like identity, payment protocols, credit, and debit.

We use Visa cards without realizing behind them is a network with protocols to protect our money.

The particular thing about these networks is that they are developed in private. Someone in the PayPal network cannot participate on the Square network. My PayPal account can't pay to your CashApp account. You can't because they are different networks.

The insight behind Strike is that the Bitcoin lightning network is the first and most efficient, cheapest, and fastest open monetary network ever created. It achieves all of these characteristics the previous networks do, like identity and payment specifications, but Strike was designed under the Bitcoin lightning network.

Jack Mallers thinks the Bitcoin lightning network plus the ACH network will outcompete the previous ones. Because it's an open network, Jack feels it gives him a competitive advantage over the other Fiat networks.

How will it work with Strike? Let's pick Martha again. Martha is in the USA, and she has a friend in the UK. She wants to send $100 to her friend.

Through Strike App, Martha will do the operation that will debit $100 from her account. Then, Strike will programmatically trade it into Bitcoin in real-time in the American lightning infrastructure to the English lightning network that converts it automatically into pounds to her friend. All of that, using Bitcoin as cash finality.

You have an asset and a monetary network that it's able to achieve cash finality anywhere in the world, at any time, at no variable cost.- Jack Mallers in What Bitcoin Did podcast.

This technique may be the ultimate breakthrough into international transaction disruption. But more than that, it can disrupt an entire sector.

The notion that we have a decentralized and open-source network makes everything possible, and if other entrepreneurs follow this innovative technique, it can potentially be the end of Visa, Mastercard, Square, and PayPal business models.

———————————— *MF* ————————————

Blessed are the meek, for they will possess the Earth.

What I think is extraordinary about Strike and Jack Mallers is his willingness to fight centralization. The way he talks in several podcasts about control and close sources made him a very libertarian entrepreneur. All he wants is to make money accessible to the entire world with the same rules.

Jack Mallers, a young bright entrepreneur from Chicago, may become one of the precursors of a unique revolution in human history.

Never before has technology made the same fair rule for the use of money reaching the entire population of planet Earth.

Mallers has a pilot project in El Salvador, but with the enthusiasm, cunning, knowledge, and willpower that Jack shows, we can be in the presence of yet another powerful phenomenon of technological disruption.

It certainly has a unique flavor, as every citizen of the world will be able, for the first time, to trade money on a fundamental pillar — the Bitcoin lightning network.

Final Thought

In an open system, winners will be companies that offer the best experience and the most attractive brand.

One day you'll go to Starbucks and find a QR code system where you can scan it with thousands of possible apps, but the winners will be the ones that treat you best, that gives you the best user experience and rewards, that are free, that over-invest in customers support, and that is most attractive.

Western nations are going to compete aggressively with each other to try to attract these technologies. If they over-regulate these companies, entrepreneurs will migrate to the best country that gives them the best choices. Why? Because this is a nomad technology.

You can create a new company using the Bitcoin lightning network in the US, but if they try to over-regulate, you can go to Portugal, the Caiman Islands, or Singapore and develop it there. It's an open-source technology, and by that, you can go to places where people embrace abundance.

Jack Millers opened the Pandora Box. He made it possible to use the Bitcoin lightning network in a way citizen from all over the world can use it to fight their fragile monetary systems.

I believe that more of these technologies will be born soon, and we can see an emergence of competitive systems that can disrupt money and give people, especially from developing countries, the opportunity to have a decent life.

Senators and politicians from the US are starting to embrace Bitcoin. I believe the USA will lead this revolution and embrace abundance, and more than that, to see the dollar increase its power. And that is good because the dollar offers peace to the world. We still have oppressive risks in the international landscape, with Russia and China trying to fight the dollar.

So, if people from Nigeria or India have a system to shift their currencies to another international currency, of course, they will choose the strongest one.

We will assist in the following decades to a massive transformation in the way we use money. People like Jack Mallers will be one of the sorcerers who create the magic formulas. Money will be dematerialized, just as Facebook did with social networks, Amazon did with retail, Apple did with mobile devices, and Tesla did with automobiles.

It's inevitable, and therefore, early adopters will undoubtedly be the winners. But above all, if the United States embraces this revolution, it will bring abundance to the entire world, that is the central premise.

Bitcoin was created to fight the disparity between rich and poor and to give equal opportunities to everyone on the planet. Many countries will try to corrupt Bitcoin.

Yet, no one will be able to defeat the code.

PART IV: WHAT A 9-PAGE WHITE PAPER DID TO THE WORLD

FROM THE HEGEMONIC PETRODOLLAR DOMINANCE TO THE AWE-INSPIRING BITCOIN STANDARD

The Petrodollars protected us from tyranny. The Bitcoin Standard will protect us from inequality.

The Triffin dilemma or Triffin paradox is the conflict of economic interests that arises between short-term domestic and long-term international objectives for countries whose currencies serve as global reserve currencies.- Wikipedia.com

In 1944, at a summit held in New Hampshire, USA, on a site called Bretton Wood, 730 delegates from all 44 allied nations at the astonishing Mount Washington Hotel joined in regulating the international monetary and financial order after World War II.

If you want to know economics, you have to understand the **United Nations Monetary and Financial Conference**, most known as the Bretton Wood agreement.

But I'm not going to bore you with historical events. You already know that President Nixon did leave the gold standard in 1971, announcing that dollars would no longer be convertible to gold, thereby putting the final nail in the coffin of the Bretton Wood's system.

However, in the 1960s, a Belgian-American economist named Robert Triffin pointed out that the country whose currency, being the global reserve currency, foreign nations wish to hold, must be willing to supply the world with an extra supply of its currency to fulfill world demand for these foreign exchange reserves, thus leading to a trade deficit.

This was called **the Triffin dilemma or Triffin paradox**:

A national currency, such as the US dollar, as a global reserve currency leads to tension between its national and international monetary policy. This is reflected in fundamental imbalances in the balance of payments, specifically the current account, as some goals require an outflow of dollars from the United States while others require an overall inflow.- Wikipedia.com

After the Vietnam War and financing the US debt, pressured by the English and the French to get back their gold, in 1971, President Nixon rejected it by announcing that the US would end the convertibility of gold.

This was the beginning of a new era. New rules, new power forces, and a system that, like all systems, have flaws.

But deep down, it's the best solution we have at the moment, until one day, forces of innovation will defeat the current system and create another system, with different rules, but also made by humans, and therefore, certainly with flaws.

———————————— *nf* ————————————

Life shouldn't be printed on dollar bills.

First, it was the colonial countries controlling the oil industry, then came the sovereign dictatorships.

I'm reading an enticing book about Calouste Gulbenkian, nicknamed "**Mr. Five Per Cent**," a British-Armenian businessman and philanthropist.

He played a significant role in making the petroleum reserves of the Middle East available to Western development and is credited with being the first person to exploit Iraqi oil.[1] Gulbenkian traveled extensively and lived in some cities, including Istanbul, London, Paris, and Lisbon.- Wikipedia.com

If you ever come to Portugal, you can't miss Calouste Gulbenkian's Foundation. The Calouste Gulbenkian Foundation was created in 1956 by the last will and testament of Calouste Sarkis Gulbenkian, a philanthropist of Armenian origin who lived in Lisbon between 1942 and the year of his death, 1955.

Yet, in the late 1950s, early 1960s, you'd had the Seven Sisters, which were the seven transnational oil companies of the "Consortium for Iran" oligopoly or cartel.

In the early 1970s, OPEC (Organization of the Petroleum Exportation Countries), led by Saudi Arabia and Qatar, manipulated the oil prices while most countries in the West ran deficits; these Arab countries amounted to biblical amounts of money.

Kissinger and Nixon had to make a move to empower again a weak dollar that lost 20% of its value against other top currencies. To get people's demand and use of the dollar, they created the petrodollar solution.

The Arabian countries had so much money they didn't know what to do with it, and the Americans needed someone to buy their debt. So, through many meetings in 1974 and 1975, Kissinger and Nixon figured out a deal that all oil sales were denominated in dollars, and with the earnings, they would buy American debt.

The Arabs had a proclivity for human rights violations and tyranny but with this kind of deal, added with weapons and protection, somehow would be found to protect mutual interests and the world to move to another level of development- pure political marketing.

This solution was so powerful that the US could print money out of thin air to buy oil, unlike Russia, which had to spend vast amounts of money to extract oil from the subsoil.

Even the fragile attempt to create the Eurodollar system fell apart, as the power of black gold in the world was already overwhelming.

———————————— *n̄f* ————————————

The aftermath of joy is not usually more joy.

Last year I read a book by a brilliant American economist called James Rickards. His book, "Aftermath: Seven Secrets of Wealth Preservation in the Coming Chaos," was an open eye for me regarding wealth preservation and how the system is built. I studied this book, and I frequently use it when I need some data about macroeconomics.

One of the most prolific ideas Rickards shared in his book was about inflation:

Critics of QE (Quantitative Easing) quickly claimed that money printing would produce a wave of inflation on this scale. Inflation never came because inflation has little to do with money supply per see. Inflation is a psychological phenomenon based on expectations and a form of adaptive behavior described mathematically as hypersynchronicity. From 2008 to 2018, that catalyst was missing because consumers were saving, paying off debt, and rebuilding their balance sheets.- James Rickards in Aftermath

Since the 1980s, the global economy has been supported by QE defended by Ben Bernanke, who served as Chair of the Federal Reserve from 2006 to 2014.

Bernanke's QE theory, called the portfolio balance channel, defended the idea that investor money has to go somewhere.

By purchasing long-term Treasury securities, the Fed lowered their total return and made them less attractive to investors. In turn, this made stocks and real estate more attractive on a relative basis. As investor funds flowed to equity and property channels, those assets would be worth more. Higher asset values would also create a wealth effect that would encourage consumption, as everyday Americans felt wealthier and more willing to spend freely. In combination, more borrowing and more spending would push inflation to the Fed's 2 percent target, facilitate normalized interest rates, and drive real GDP growth to its former self-sustaining trend above 3 percent. None of these results emerged.- James Rickards in Aftermath

In reality, the real GDP growth from June 2009 to the first quarter of 2018 was less than 2.2 percent, entirely below the long-term trend.

Actually, QE and zero rates did have one fantastic effect- they created asset bubbles.

Fed governors also live in a bubble. They persist in their reliance on the

Phillips Curve, which predicts that low unemployment leads to rising inflation.

Yet, the Phillips Curve bears no correspondence to reality. The 1960s were characterized by low unemployment and rising inflation. The late 1970s were characterized by high unemployment and high inflation. The 2010s have been characterized by low unemployment and low inflation. There is no correlation between inflation and money supply. Inflation is always and everywhere a psychological phenomenon. When citizens lose confidence in the form of money, velocity takes off. Reliance on the Phillips Curve for Fed policymakers is false science.- James Rickards in Aftermath

Again, pure political marketing sharing confidence that the US economy is on a solid growth path.

You are imperfect permanently and inevitably flawed.

The monetary system that has been built by Alan Greenspan and Ben Bernanke and now by Jerome Powell has not solved inequality globally, nor in the USA.

The US dollar is most used for political purposes, and that's comprehensive since geopolitical forces try to gain preponderance, some of which are tyrannical and dictatorial forces.

In that respect, the dollar has been a safety plug. But we have not yet managed to devise a system that allows politicians to operate in a balanced way the propensity to increase debts, with aspects of inequality.

This system is more than proven that it can try to solve geopolitical threats, but not even in the United States itself does it solve the constraints of inequalities.

In the last two decades, for growth to occur at a global stage, to produce 46 trillion dollars of GDP, the world created 182 trillion dollars in debt. The global economy shouldn't rely on politicians to manage the real economy. They don't have the knowledge to know the supply and demand complexity issues of global markets.

However, what politicians want at all costs is to avoid another collapse. But for that to happen, they create a massively huge asset bubble that one day will burst. Why? Have you ever heard the expression: nobody serves free lunches?

The thing is that the monetary system isn't transparent. We actually don't know what central banks and governments do behind doors. And by being opaque, one day when the system starts failing, confidence in the system also fails, and people will start saving, not consuming, and paying their debts.

In a system that needs to create debt like a drug addict needs another dose, when there is not enough debt created, the deck of cards collapses.

———————— nF ————————

The Bitcoin Standard will protect us from inequality.

There is a phenomenon called **Dutch disease**, which is a concept that describes an economic phenomenon where the rapid development of one sector of the economy precipitates a decline in other sectors.

This concept describes how some countries export a lot of a commodity; it cannibalized the other sectors of the economy. In this case, the commodity that the USA exported was the US dollar.

When the US issues massive amounts of the global reserve currency, the other countries have to acquire a lot of it to engage in the worldwide commerce, and it causes profoundly impacted trading constraints.

Now, the USA has a complex problem to solve, a massive trade deficit to manage, as in the early 1970s, because of a lack of production capacity. Biden's administration has a 6 trillion-dollar bazooka to anticipate future constraints on this matter, but the question is: is it too late?

People in Cambodia or El Salvador still prefer the dollar to their current currency, and the US dollar is still a powerful tool that stabilizes poor countries, but that's a minor consequence of the existing monetary system. It still doesn't create enough wealth for those people's countries to solve their financial problems.

The crypto industry may have that capacity, with a crypto dollar being a faster, more accessible, and transparent tool globally. Meaning, stable coins may ideally be the perfect boost to developed countries to build wealth and create new jobs, industries, and competitiveness.

Bitcoin may become the monetary good, shortly, at the very top of the money hierarchy, and adopted by several countries. The advantage the Bitcoin has compared to gold is that it can't be confiscated like colonial countries did in the 1920s or the US in the post-World War II.

The other advantage is that the new monetary system could be collateralized by the Bitcoin, which would create a more verifiable, transparent, and equal system. As a matter of fact, it would empower the dollar more efficiently as an anti-fragile new digital entity.

We have another shoot here, where we can create a new system the ultimate monetary good is less centralized and less confiscatable. It could look like a kind of Bretton Wood system, where you could have the dollar and a hand of other currencies still be powerful, but they would be pegs to the Bitcoin at some rate.- Alex Gladstein, the Chief
Strategy Officer at The Human Rights Foundation

Final Thoughts

Developed countries can have a huge bonus now if they embrace the Bitcoin Standard before others. They can start mining Bitcoin to attract Bitcoin mining companies and the all-new industry and be early adopters.

No one knows what's going to happen in the post-petrodollar era.

Yet, the petrodollar and weaponized geopolitical experiment had been poorly efficient.

I think the US will no longer need the petrodollar hegemony to fight inequality. If the dollar becomes weaker, the US exports will boost again. And in a technological deflationary decade ahead, high rates of unemployment and an American 2.0 industrial renaissance would boost the western countries again.

The Bitcoin Standard, from a monetary perspective, can be beneficial; like in the 1970s, the gold was, with its intrinsic volatility, before it becomes mainstream.

Like gold, Bitcoin has the potential to be a very quality commodity, with its volatile characteristics, very common in these kinds of hard assets.

It took thousands of years for global society to achieve the price discovery on a commodity like gold. I don't think the price discovery will take that long for Bitcoin to occur, as its characteristics, in a supersonic world, could resolve this issue in less than a decade.

The price discovery of Bitcoin is entering its second decade. Big corporations are starting to realize that Bitcoin is a good thing to have. You have Ray Dalio, Stanley Druckenmiller, and Paul Tudor Jones. Most recently, Kevin O'Leary and Carl Icahn joined the Bitcoin network.

From a global adoption of 2% to 10 or 20%, we'll observe short volatility in the Bitcoin market. But if people keep adopting Bitcoin, I don't see why it shouldn't be the ultimate monetary good.

For the US government, I have the feeling that it's going to be a great solution. For the central banks and their opaque transparency, I doubt.

America is prepared like never before for the Bitcoin Standard. They have the right people in the country's leadership, infrastructures, mining users, developers, holdings, brokerages, and the industry is in great shape.

America is in a prime position to lead the Bitcoin Standard to the future.

CENTRAL BANKS LOOMING ASSAULT TO MANIPULATE BITCOIN

What is their ultimate game plan?

"Bitcoin is a highly speculative asset, which has conducted some funny business and some interesting and totally reprehensible money laundering activity," Christine Lagarde said in January 2021 in an interview at the Reuters Next conference.

In 2012, seven percent of bitcoin transactions did happen for criminal deals. Currently, the percentage dropped to less than one percent.

The utility of bitcoin has grown well beyond its use for criminal purposes.

In June 2019, the G20 planned to remove anonymity from the crypto space. They formed the Financial Action Task Force's (FATF). Crypto exchanges would keep detailed information of all senders and receivers. In the name of cutting down on criminal activities.

We can use any tool for good or bad. And criminal control activity is essential for a healthy democracy.

Yet, if you compare one percent of bitcoin to what happens in the global financial system, you'd find Christine Lagarde's comments at least intriguing.

2–5% of global GDP ($800 billion — $2 trillion) do money laundering each year using the dollar.

Some commentators argue that financial institutions are not doing enough to stop money laundering and are instead filing SARs to protect themselves from criminal prosecution while profiting from processing suspicious transactions.- jdsupra.com

Deutsch Bank and JPMorgan Chase are some of the top banks flagged in fraud. A cache of leaked documents shows years of transactions handled by the world's largest banks linked to money laundering, corruption, and fraud.

2.7 trillion dollars in money laundering is a bunch of money. And these banks are linked to these terrible accusations. But no, that's not the issue. Let's get the attention to bitcoin, which has a market cap of a couple of billion dollars.

On 20th December 2016, BBC News reported,

A French court has found International Monetary Fund chief Christine Lagarde guilty of negligence but did not hand down any punishment.

As French finance minister in 2008, she approved an award of €404m ($429m; £340m) to businessman Bernard Tapie for the disputed sale of a firm.

I guess everyone has their hands dirty, doesn't it, madame Lagarde?

— *nf* —

That Government Is Best Which Governs Least

The governments can't stop bitcoin, but they can put you in prison or fine you if you own it.

It all leads to **capital control** definition,

Capital control represents any measure taken by a government, central bank, or other regulatory body to limit foreign capital flow in and out of the domestic economy. These controls include taxes, tariffs, legislation, volume restrictions, and market-based forces. Capital controls can affect many asset classes such as equities, bonds, and foreign exchange trades.- Investopedia

This concept is recent in history because, in the last century, there were few international transactions. So there was no need for governments to control capital transactions.

After the First Great War, many countries found themselves in bankruptcy. Or had to print large amounts of money, devaluing their currencies.

In many cases, wealthy people tried to get their fortunes out of the country. Those same countries prevented that from happening. They created legislation and taxes for those who wanted to get their money out.

In 1944, after the Second Great War, with the Bretton Wood agreement, the capital was allowed to be used for international trade. Only for goods and services. So, you still couldn't take your wealth and put it in another country.

Yet, in 1971, Nixon ends the convertibility of US dollars to gold, which brought an end to Bretton Wood's agreement.

Capital control was always the ultimate tool from governments and central banks to dominate the system's money flow.

That's why ECB and IMF are starting to go public about Bitcoin and other cryptocurrencies — dominating capital control.

———————————— *nF* ————————————

What the Global Regulators Are Saying

When we talk about regulators, all eyes go to the US Federal Reserve. They are the ones who dictate the rules worldwide. Since more than 70% of global transactions are made in dollars.

Brian P. Brooks became Acting Comptroller of the Currency until January 14, 2021. As Acting Comptroller of the Currency, Mr. Brooks was the administrator of the federal banking system. And the chief officer of the Office of the Comptroller of the Currency (OCC).

The OCC supervises nearly 1,200 national banks, federal savings associations, federal branches, and foreign bank agencies that conduct approximately 70% of all banking business in the United States. The OCC's mission is to ensure that national banks and federal savings associations operate in a safe and sound manner, provide fair access to financial services, treat customers fairly, and comply with applicable laws and regulations.-occ.treas.gov

In a recent interview at CNBC, Brooks declared,

"We're very focused on getting this right. We are very focused on not killing this, and it is equally important that we develop the networks behind Bitcoin and other cryptos as it is we prevent money laundering and terrorism financing."

A few weeks later, the OCC announced that federally chartered banks and thrifts may participate in independent node verification networks. And use stable coins for payment activities.

This was seen as essential news in the crypto world.

In many cases, the financial system has the most powerful lobbyists. And they are frequently accused of writing the bills themselves. Cryptocurrencies will be the new reality in the American financial system. Sooner than we think.

—————————— *nF* ——————————

Final Thoughts

Some have predicted that the Great Reset is close.

Others see it as a unique opportunity for all central banks 'to clean all the mess.

Meanwhile, stable coins are coming. Bitcoin gets serious as a hard asset, with companies starting to pill up BTCs as a refugee asset for their portfolio.

And a consequential technology disruption breaks out with Tesla leading the way. The fintech is already boosting to a radical shift in the banking industry. And genomics is close to revolutionizing the entire health sector.

It seems like the perfect storm is coming.

For more than 100 years, we assisted to a slow evolution of the last technology disruption. It enabled us to have electricity, a telephone, and an internal combustion engine at our disposal.

Now, we have artificial intelligence, deep learning, and genomics.

We also have cryptocurrencies, streaming, self-driving cars, cloud computing, and energy storage. All these technologies are invading our homes.

I think we're a privileged generation. I'm enjoying millions to have the chance to analyze great companies and technologies.

If you are like me, a compulsive optimistic, you'll feel the same vibe.

Let us see what the next episodes will bring us.

A great reset? A Bitcoin regulation? Tech companies destroying postindustrial revolution industries?

It's like predicting the stock market.

I don't know. You don't know. Nobody knows.

Stay safe and enjoy the journey.

BITCOIN FOR BILLIONS, NOT FOR BILLIONIRES: THE STAGGERING STORY OF THE LIGHTNING NETWORK WORLDWIDE

Charity Water project will disrupt mindsets all over the world.

Scott Harrison was born in the suburbs of New York City in a happy family until one day his mother collapsed on the bedroom floor. Harrison was four years old at that time, and his mother suffered from a carbon monoxide gas leak, and her immune system died that day.

She became allergic to everything, and she had to wear strange masks often connected to oxygen all the time.

After the poisoning, Scott Harrison had to help his father doing a little of everything at home. He had to take care of his mother for his father to pay the bills with his job and side-hustles.

Harrison was a good Christian kid who played the piano at the church and wanted to be a doctor when he grew up to help sick people like his mother.

Then, he became an adolescent.

He moved to New York, joined a music band, and then became a nightclub promoter. He managed to arrange beautiful and rich people for parties and charge $500 a bottle of champagne that cost $40.

From club to club, alcohol and drugs, beautiful women, a Rolex in his wrist, and ten years smocking two packs of cigarettes a night, strip clubs, and gambling, Harrison seemed to have lost his way.

At one particular party in Uruguay, in an incredible house near the beach, expensive champagne, amazing dancers, and massive production, a long decline in happiness starts to invade Harrison's soul.

I tried to find my way back to very lost faith.- Scott Harrison

To compensate for his lack of happiness, he sold everything he had and took a year off, trying to find his mean of helping others instead of himself.

He tried to apply to various humanitarian organizations, but nobody wanted him. They didn't even want him volunteering.

Fortunately, one organization said if Scott would pay $500 a month, he could join them.

A fantastic team of doctors and surgeons who travel the world in a hospital ship specialized in removing face tumors accepted Scott. They went into Liberia, one of the poorest countries in the world.

As Harrison went to some villages, he started to see how locals drink water. They literally drunk water from swamps full of mosquitoes and bugs. Most kids die before they were 10 years old of cholera or diarrhea and other infectious diseases.

785 million people live on our planet without access to clean water.

So, Harrison started to do what he does best. He came back to New York and began organizing parties. But this time, charging money to finance his new project.

Charity Water started on his 31st birthday party, with 700 people spending money to raise $15,000. They immediately took that money to Northern Uganda, built three wells, and then sent back photos of the water infrastructure in those villages providing clean water back to those 700 people.

Most western country citizens don't trust charities, but this way of doing things was utterly disrupted. If you donate to Charity Water, you can track your money, you can see what country and village your money goes to.

And that was a game-changer.

———————————— *nF* ————————————

Quality improves with effort accordingly to an exponential curve.

One day, Scott Harrison was in a charity event, and one of his donators wanted to donate in Bitcoin. So, Harrison received a 559 Bitcoin donation that he sold the next day for 4.4 million dollars. Yet, if he'd keep it and sold it in April 2021, it would worth 35 million dollars.

With all that 559 Bitcoin, Charity Water helped more than 100,000 people, but they could help six to nine hundred thousand human beings if they've kept the Bitcoin a little while.

In 2021, Scott Harrison is managing a 100-million-dollar charity that helps two million people worldwide, and now he's having a problem when he receives Bitcoin instead of dollars.

Could the charity keep the asset and benefit from its appreciation? Should they borrow in dollars collateralizing their Bitcoins?

Harrison started to talk with some staff members to find a way to hodl their Bitcoin, meaning to keep Bitcoin to appreciate in a certain amount of time. That's where they decided they would keep all Bitcoin (hodl) until 2025.

There's a risk in this strategy. If Bitcoin loses value until 2025, at that time, Charity Water will help fewer people than it would help today. Charities never do that. Yet, charities never had to deal with this kind of situation before.

In 14 years, Scott Harrison raised an impressive 550 million dollars in donations. Charity Water helped 12 million people having clean water since day one. Yet, it's 1.6% of the global problem.

But from rapid acceleration to exponential growth, Harrison knows that it's a huge difference because he understands the network effect Bitcoin has.

Bitcoin could provide a unique exponential story for Charity Water.

In a US dollar structure, Charity Water is about to build a trust fund to hodl Bitcoin. And as it will hopefully appreciate over time, as it is in its early adoption worldwide, Harrison will be able to exponentially build not 10 wells but 1,000 wells in 2025.

So he will help not 1.6% of people who don't have clean water, but 10% or more. So 10% of 785 million people is 78.5 million human beings drinking clean water.

That's almost the entire population of Germany.

———————— $\mathscr{NF}$ ————————

Lightning makes no sound until it strikes.

The Bitcoin lightning network is the most inclusive monetary network of all time. Why? Simple. Can a citizen of El Salvador or Venezuela use a Visa or Mastercard free of charge or without being subjected to such a violent exchange that leaves them with no money to spend? No.

The Bitcoin lightning network works in El Salvador as well as in Chicago, Lisbon, or Sydney. That's why it's the most inclusive network.

Yet, this doesn't have any significance for rich countries like the US, UK, France, or Australia. As people drinking water from swamps, the problem is so far away, it looks like it's no problem at all.

Having the dollar and the euro system working smoothly in our countries, most of us don't realize 3/4 of the world doesn't have this kind of privilege.

You don't have dirty water for your kids to drink, the same way you don't have your currency so devalued you never make it out of the poverty line.

You and I don't have this kind of problem, so we internalize they don't exist.

However, **785 million people**, two times the size of the entire US population, don't have clean water to drink. Currently, **two billion people** worldwide cannot access financial services because their data is not held on 'traditional' sources.

What if the Bitcoin Lightning network would solve part of that problem?

Most recently, I wrote an article about Jack Mallers, a young entrepreneur that created Strike, an open-source payment system developed in the lightning network that permits anyone with a phone device to download an app, create a wallet, and buy, sell, or hodl Bitcoin, at the speed of light, with almost no fees.

El Salvador and Tanzania recently adopted Bitcoin as legal tender to create a new economy, the one that can access the US dollar and the euro, like any other western citizens, but with a unique tool- using only their phone.

I hope technology and innovation reach the poorest people. Frankly, I don't give a sheet about the rich countries; they have minor problems, while 3/4 of the world is fighting for survival.

---------- *nF* ----------

Final Thoughts

While rich countries play power games, debating whether Bitcoin is an asset or not, 3/4 of the world fights for survival.

While the United States and Europe are concerned about inflation, 3/4 of the world is worried about diseases transmitted by polluted water.

While the world of the rich thinks it has the right to luxury hospitals and roads, 3/4 of the world struggles to have dignity in their daily lives.

This is the real problem with money.

There is too much money in rich countries, making them immoral, rotten, and cynical. While 3/4 of the world is short of cash, making it fragile, hopeless, and hungry.

Over 45,000 people die of starvation, 38,000 of them children, every single day.

There's something fundamentally wrong in our planet, in our morality, inside our brains.

When I listen to Scott Harrison or Jack Mallers, I see hope because they give me the notion of how lucky I am to live in a European country, where I can raise my daughters in clean water and a secure environment.

Yet, what kind of morality do I have in a world where 45-year-old fathers don't have the same luxury?

EL SALVADOR ADOPTED BITCOIN NOT FOR THE REASONS SOME PEOPLE THINK THEY DID

The lack of knowledge leads to a lack of well-founded news.

The estimated amount of money laundered globally in one year is 2– 5% of global GDP, or $800 billion — $2 trillion in current US dollars. Due to the clandestine nature of money laundering, it is however difficult to estimate the total amount of money that goes through the laundering cycle.- unodc.org

Many politicians have been accused Bitcoin of being used for illicit transactions, which made me search for money laundering history.

I found that in 2009, the year that the Bitcoin was created, 80% of trade finance was conducted in USD. And a report estimated that in 2009, criminal proceeds amounted to 3.6% of global GDP, with 2.7% (or USD 1.6 trillion) being laundered.

I kept digging and found another interesting piece of data:

The report cited documents leaked by BuzzFeed News that identified more than $2 trillion in transactions between 1999 and 2017 that were flagged by financial institutions' internal compliance officers as possible money laundering or other criminal activity, including $514 billion at JPMorgan and $1.3 trillion at Deutsche Bank.- thestreet.com

Money laundering has been used with the compliance of commercial banks for decades, as exposed by BuzzFeedNews.

Yet, I found that the real problem about money laundering and illicit transactions doesn't have anything to do with Bitcoin.

Bitcoin is a new technology, and obviously, those who do illicit actions will try to use this new technology to keep their activities. Some blockchains were created for scams, but developers and coders used tools to mitigate the problem.

As legitimate cryptocurrency use goes up, crypto crime as a percentage goes down. 2020 crypto crime was down 57% from 2019, dropping from $4.5 billion to $1.9 billion in 2020.- ciphertrace.com

The problem of money laundering is much more complex, and we could be talking about this issue for weeks.

What I find challenging is listening to politicians sharing their concerns about Bitcoin and its illicit transactions when the primary problem is in the US dollar system. To be intellectually honest, people should address illegal transactions more broadly.

El Salvador recently adopted Bitcoin as legal tender, and the newspapers and anti-bitcoiners jumped right in to criticize Bitcoin volatility, arguing it will destroy El Salvador's economy.

Again, people don't know what they're talking about if they don't study the subjects.

El Salvador will use the Lightning Network payments platform, Strike, created by the entrepreneur Jack Mallers, to protect their wealth against the monetary expansion of the US dollar that will end up with most foreign currencies around the world.

But what is the Lightning Network, and how can it help developed countries protect themselves from the American monetary expansion?

———————————— *nF* ————————————

Lightning makes no sound until it strikes.

The Lightning Network is a new digital bearing instrument that cares physical value to achieve transaction finality at any time, at no cost, anywhere on the planet.

Bitcoin as an asset class has sufficient liquidity in every currency so that Bitcoin and its satoshis belong to these infrastructures where the Lightning Network effectively works.

Imagine these little satoshis (1 Bitcoin is equivalent to 100,000,000 satoshis) being sent around like soldiers.

If I want to send one thousand dollars to a friend of mine in the UK, my euros will convert into these little satoshis (soldiers). They run out to the UK, and the Lightning Network will convert these soldiers into British pounds at no cost at the speed of light.

The intelligent system uses the 24/7, 365 totally availability and liquidity to swap any kind of currency.

Imagine if my friend in the UK needs to send 100 pounds to El Salvador. The Lightning Network converts 100 pounds into satoshis, and then those same satoshis swap into El Salvador's cólons.

The fact that I'm using euros and my friend is using pounds is pure convenience. And that's the true disruptive power of the Lightning Network.

———————————— *nF* ————————————

I prefer dangerous freedom over peaceful slavery.

The United States of America had expanded its money supply by over 30% last year.

However, the money supply expansion is governed by a law called the **Law of Acceleration of Issuance and Depreciation.**

The Law of Acceleration of Issuance and Depreciation tells us the more money you print, the more money later you have to print, just to keep the system going.

Accelerated depreciation methods tend to align the recognized rate of an asset's depreciation with its actual use, although this isn't technically required. This alignment tends to occur because an asset is most heavily used when it's new, functional, and most efficient.- investopedia.com

The expansion on the money supply M2 will double in the next four years, and it will double again and again. And in this depreciation process, many of the weaker currencies will collapse.

From 100 trillion dollars of money printing in the M2, we'll expect by the end of 2030 1.25 quadrillion US dollars to be printed in a massive depreciation tsunami that will end up with most foreign currencies worldwide.

In this process, the Bitcoin adoption will also be massive from developed countries to defend themselves from the American expansion policy.

As a finite asset, Bitcoin will appreciate in a counter cycle to the American monetary expansion. It will bring more opportunities for the Lightning Network and the blockchain industry to evolve and create new innovative markets.

What about the US dollar?

Well, listen to what Jeff Booth said in his book The Price of Tomorrow:

(…)delivering the newly created money into the economy, is done in a variety of ways, such as large-scale asset purchases from public and private sectors like the Troubled Asset Relief Program, where the government buys toxic or underperforming assets. By doing so, governments take bad assets off the balance sheets of corporations and give them fresh capital instead.

—————————————— *nf* ——————————————

Final Thoughts

Monetary expansion from all central banks in the world should scare everyone that have some knowledge about finance.

This experience of global monetary expansion is bringing new and challenging problems to modern society. More inequality, difficult access for most countries globally to the dollar and the euro, and above all, it seems to be dragging the sovereign debt problem indefinitely in a kind of Ponzi scheme.

There are countries like El Salvador and, more recently, Tanzania that have already realized the power of a scarce asset like Bitcoin. They've also learned that the Lightning Network is a technology that can give them almost unrestricted access to the financial market, finally putting them on an equal footing with the western world.

But other risks could arise since the dollar and the euro are not just currencies; they are geopolitical tools that staunch many of the potential dangers that extreme ideologies can bring to the global world.

The financial world is in perfect turmoil, and in the coming decades, we will have the marking of firm positions on the part of countries like Russia and China, the United States, and the UK, which may dictate the future of exchanges globally.

Developed countries just want to survive and have dignity, which they don't have in the current financial system.

The great and powerful countries want to continue their hegemony in foreign policy. But a new invisible force, driven by the blockchain's technological disruption, is turning the world around.

Decentralized financial institutions threaten commercial banks; sectors are being entirely disrupted by the power of new networks, tokens, and blockchains.

The gamification of the entire economy has started. Communities and tokens will operate in a decentralized system, trusted by smart contracts, in an open-source environment.

Third parties will be decimated by a peer-to-peer new philosophy of doing business.

The Lightning Network is just one of the infinite tools that will operate in this decentralized economy.

As more regulation arises, the more mature and secure the new system becomes, finding bridges between the analogic world and the digital one.

In this transition, I hope the system can regenerate itself without too much damage. What we've seen in the Great Recession of 2008 is nothing compared with the risks that the economy presents today.

Governments worldwide are trying to understand the potential of Bitcoin and the blockchain in the future design of a modern economy.

Central bankers don't want to lose power, and they are getting much more aggressive.

The power of technology will keep pressuring into a deflationary environment, while the monetary expansion tries to further push debt cycles.

El Salvador embraced the Bitcoin network because they don't want to be hostage to the analog system. They know what comes next, and they want to anticipate as early adopters.

If it will work? Only the future knows.

The only thing I know is that we live in extraordinary times. I look like a front-line spectator seeing Michael Jordan flying in the Chicago Arena.

Humans have the power to figure out ways to make things work.

I still believe in human ingenuity. I'm just not sure if it will help the Lightning Network to thrive in a global decentralized and trustful economy.

Sitting in the front line, I'll wait and see who's going to fly higher.

WARREN BUFFETT VS. THE BLOCKCHAIN NETWORK: A DEEP REFLECTION OF A TRANSITION MINDSET

How Warren Buffet managed money in the past. How money should be managed in the future.

His skill is investing, but his secret is time.- Morgan Housel in The Psychology of Money: Timeless lessons on wealth, greed, and happiness.

Warren Buffett's net worth is $84.5 billion. Yet, $84.2 billion was accumulated after his 50th birthday.

Don't forget the first phrase His skill is investing, but his secret is time because if Buffett were an ordinary investor when he was 30 years old and had a net worth of $9.3 million, like most investors, he could have been enjoying life, his family, his friends, like a regular guy.

Imagine if Buffett would spend some money on a boat, admirable propriety, traveling around the world, and in his 30s, he would end up with $25,000. Yet, imagine he would still keep his extraordinary annual investment return of 22% but stopped investing and retired at age 60.

His estimated net worth would be $11.9 million. 99% less net worth than it is today.

More than 2,000 books were written about Warren Buffett's incredible skills, yet nobody shared his most crucial skill of all- time.

Jim Simmons has compounded money at 66% annually since 1988. He was probably the best investor of all time. However, even compounding a third of that, Warren accumulated $84.5 billion against $21 billion from Simons. Why? Because Simons started when he was at age 50.

The magic of compounding interests is so powerful over time that the annual average return turns into a secondary factor. Read that again.

We were educated to think in a linear perspective, not an exponential one;

that's why we usually do easy math like 8+8+8+8+8 but struggle to do 8x8x8x8.

IBM created its first hard drive with 3.5 megabytes in the 1950s. In the 1970s, IBM held a 70 megabytes hard drive. In 1999, Apple came with a 6-gigabyte hard drive. In 2006, Apple reached 250 gigs on the new iMac. In 2019, we saw personal computers with 100 terabyte hard drives.

From 1950 to 1990, hard drive capacity increased by 296 megabytes. From 1990 through the present day, we gained 100 million megabytes.

Now you can understand the power of compounding interests and why Warren Buffett won the race against every single investor in the world. From his 17 years old to his 91, he just had to wait for the exponential curve to take effect.

That makes us think that our effort to beat the market or trying to find in the endless books written (I bought three of them) about Buffett's techniques is a waste of time.

If you put a portion of your money from an early age into the S&P500 index with a 10% annual return since its inception in 1926, and you use time to your advantage, you don't need to be a mathematic genius to be fine at 65.

We should take some time to think about what's enough for us. This word is compelling in the investment world because it all comes down to the magic number you want to achieve. Is it $1 million? $2.5 million? $10 million? $1 billion?

Enough is realizing that the opposite- an insatiable appetite for more- will push you to the point of regret.- Morgan Housel in The Psychology of Money: Timeless lessons on wealth, greed, and happiness.

———————————— *nf* ————————————

I'm not a macroeconomics person.

No single piece of macroeconomic advice given by the expert to their government has ever had the results predicted.- Peter Drucker.

Since the 1970s, long-run growth rates have quickly declined and leveled off at around 3 percent per year for the following three decades. Then, growth contracted again sharply and has been declining ever since.

Another critical factor that we must know is that the robotization of the entire economy is taking place. That means that robots will take most of our jobs.

Don't worry, the world is not going to end, not that I know.

The analog world will be dismantled into a new world, with disruptive industries rising. And for that to happen, we'll need millions of workers to reshape the new economy. Robots will not be able to do all the work, but they will help us have a better life.

The global economy is changing and is changing fast. The pandemic just boosted the shift. Most workers do their job at home now, in a more efficient way.

Self-driving cars are being tested, artificial intelligence is working in thousands of devices that help us in our daily routines.

The digitization of the entire economy is taking place.

And one of the last industries that were held to the analog world was the financial system. But not anymore.

Central banks are incrementing their power over money. As a result, central bank digital currency, or the so-called CBDCs, will do most commercial banks' work, but more efficiently.

Money will be totally digitized into wallets that will guide your financial routines in an ultra-efficient machine, highly centralized and regulated.

For the ordinary individual, it will be better, cheaper, and userfriendly. In addition, technology will help people to manage their financial behavior.

However, the global economy will have to deal with one big problem- debt.

Most experts believe that a Great Reset has to be done because with the technological deflationary pressure, inflation will be impossible to manage, and central banks will need to print exponential amounts of money to pay the previous debts in a vicious cycle.

Important international agreements will have to be made, with the power of different currencies be negotiated at the G7 table to create a new basket to currencies with different weights.

The million-dollar question is: what will happen during the transition?

———————————— *nf* ————————————

The struggle between centralization and decentralization is at the core of American history.

After the 2008 Great Recession, an anonymous individual or group of individuals created a 9-page white paper that quickly spread all over the internet.

Millions of people talk about that name- Satoshi Nakamoto. In the 9page white paper was mentioned:

A purely peer-to-peer version of electronic cash would allow online payments to be sent directly from one party to another without going through a financial institution. Digital signatures provide part of the solution, but the main benefits are lost if a trusted third party is still required to prevent double-spending.

12 years later, the Lightning Network allows an individual to exchange their country's currency for dollars through a simple mobile phone, almost free, at the speed of light, without a trusted third party. I guess technology and decentralization won.

The question about the Bitcoin network and all the industry of decentralized finance (DeFi) and the endless blockchains already created is if it's going to have enough power to spread worldwide and be part of the daily routine of most human beings?

It's a genuine question because central banks and Western governments don't want to lose their geopolitical power. But, on the other hand, companies and countries have already adopter the Bitcoin network. Companies like Tesla and Microstrategy, American states like Wyoming and Texas, countries like El Salvador and Tanzania are at the beginning of this massive adoption.

The centralized world wants the magic tool to print money to keep the power of manipulating currencies and "free" markets.

The decentralized world wants the market to work free of manipulations, the price discovery to get track again, and the individual to be free to decide which currency is best for its own interest- therefore, to really democratize the finance worldwide.

Seeing the massive adoption of the Bitcoin network worldwide and seeing western countries starting to realize some usage of the Bitcoin network, can we find a new macroeconomic ecosystem that brings the best of both worlds?

Final Thoughts

I just bought $2,000 of Bitcoin, but also $2,500 of Apple stocks.

Will Apple stocks be collateralized by the Bitcoin network in the future? Will Bitcoin replace gold as a new reserve currency? How can a Great Reset happen without the entire collapse of the markets?

If I was in 1950, it would be easier because the world wasn't being threatened by a gigantic snowball of debt and a new decentralized financial technology.

The best thing is to be on both sides of the bridge.

I'm not an absolutist about Bitcoin. But I am a severe critic of the current financial system. I know it's the best system have, but we need to be better.

The market has not been free for a long time, and no one with good judgment is interested in a Marxist regime again, are we?

His skill is investing, but his secret is time.

As I have nowhere else to go, and a portion of my money is in the stock market, another in real estate, and another in Bitcoin, I guess all I have to do is keep investing and hope that luck and time can do their magic thing of compounding my assets.

I don't live in Omaha, and I'm not 17 years old, but I have two beautiful daughters and a legacy to defend.

On the other hand, I feel privileged to be passing through this generation with so many challenges ahead related to climate change, the robotization of the economy, the disruption of money, and all the micro-phenomena that are happening in our everyday.

Having the privilege of writing and sharing ideas in this challenging time is a source of pride for me.

Having readers and writers who challenge me every day to think and reflect deeply makes me a more complete person.

Time, this powerful entity, will dictate what the future holds.

I already know that I have to have patience and an exponential look at the world because it seems that we will start a new era at the speed of light.

IF YOU DON'T UNDERSTAND THE INFINITE GAME YOU'LL BELIEVE THE BITCOIN NETWORK WILL FALL

From the hegemony of Fiat currencies to the Bitcoin network.

In the early 1900s, a group of highly funded experts stood ready for one of humanity's most significant challenges.

Samuel Pierpont Langley publicly declared that he would be the first man to fly an airplane. Langley was a highly regarded man at the Smithsonian Institution, professor of mathematics, and a lecturer at Harvard.

Among his wealthy friends were names like Andrew Carnegie and Alexander Graham Bell. Langley even received a $50,000 grant from the US War Department. With a team with all the resources, its success was guaranteed.

A few hundred miles away, Wilbur and Orville Wright were inventing their own flying machine. Their passion for flying was so intense that the small community they lived in got involved in helping them with the impossible task. But, unfortunately, there was no funding, no government support, no contacts at the highest level, and no graduates in their work team.

However, in an old bicycle shop, the community began work on the plane project.

On December 17, 1903, that particular community witnessed the first man fly for the first time in human history.

How did the Wright brothers manage to reach their goal, without any conditions whatsoever, and the so famous and highly financed Langley did not? It wasn't luck.

Both were highly motivated. Both had excellent scientific experience and professional ethics.

But the Wright brothers started with **why**!

Finite game vs. Infinite game.

According to James Carse, there are at least two kinds of games; the finite games and the infinite games.

A finite game is played for the purpose of winning, an infinite game for the purpose of continuing the play.- James Carse

In his brilliant book Start With Why, Simon Sinek explained his vision about the finite and infinite game.

Sinek explained there is no such thing as winning marriage, or business, or global politics. We're constantly playing infinite games in our lives. But if you listen to many leaders, they always say they've won, are the number one, or are the best.

The question is: based on what?

There are no metrics, no time frames to measure who wins what, where, and when. Meaning, most of us are playing the infinite game with a finite mindset.

Yet, if you play the game with the wrong rules, something happens.

If you play the infinite game with a finite mindset, there are apparent outcomes. The decline of trust, a decline of cooperation, and the decline of innovation.

One perfect example that Simon Sinek shared was when he spoke to an education summit at Microsoft and a meeting for Apple.

At the Microsoft summit, the majority of the executives spend almost the entire time speaking about how to beat Apple.

At the Apple meeting, everybody in the room spends all their time talking about how to help teachers teach and help students learn.

One was obsessed with where they were going, the other one was obsessed with beating their competition.

Microsoft, with its finite mindset, was struggling.

After the presentation, Microsoft gave him the new Zune, the last tech gadget from Microsoft, in response to the iPod.

After the Apple presentation, Sinek shared a taxi with a senior Apple executive, and he couldn't help himself. He said to the Apple executive: Microsoft gave me the new Zune. It's so much better than your iPod touch.

The Apple executive turned to Sinek and responded: I have no doubt. And the conversation was over.

When someone is playing with the infinite mindset, they know that sometimes you have the better product, and sometimes somebody else has a better product. So there's no such thing as winning or losing; there's no such thing as being the best.

There's only **ahead** or **behind**.

The goal of the infinite game is not to beat the competition. Instead, the goal is to outlast the competition.

———————————— *NF* ————————————

First, know what money is, then find your own purpose for it.

I recently wrote an article where I resume the history of money and where I think the financial world tends to go. But I don't have certainties of any kind, as I believe none of us have. Nobody can predict the future. We can only observe, describe, and eventually bet in favor of something we believe in.

I shared this thought in that article:

Money as a technological tool is being redesigned as we speak. The Federal Reserve, the European Central Bank, and the Bank of China are all working hard to take advantage of the cryptographic innovation that started with a simple 9-page-white-paper.

I don't see myself as a Bitcoin maximalist, but I confess I was somehow biased and somewhat aggressive in my words against the Fiat economic system.

Last year, I read many books describing how the financial world has been built, with governments, central banks, and commercial banks managing money in ways that put more money in the pocket of the few.

I know that Winston Churchill said Democracy is the worst form of government except for the others. And he was right on that statement.

However, as I write about the Fiat system and the Bitcoin network, I feel a lack of common sense. And I assume I've been in that category too.

Most Bitcoin maximalists go public on Twitter only talking about how BTC is going to the moon, sharing graphics and empty words instilling people to buy the crypto today to a get-rich-quick moment.

Like Anthony Pompliano, Preston Pysh, Raoul Pal, and Jeff Booth, only a few have the clairvoyance to share what is really happening behind the scenes in the Bitcoin Network.

These Bitcoin believers have been interviewing developers, coders, entrepreneurs, and even politicians that are really working hard to provide another financial structure in a decentralized network managed by code, protocols, and smart contracts.

On the other hand, central banks and governments are living in challenging times, with debts rising, inflation rising, and the gap between the richest and the poorest increasing.

The morality of the present financial system is being under pressure.

To some extent, information is now running at high speed, and the population is beginning to understand how money is created. Ordinary citizens also understand who creates it and where it is being channeled. In fact, this is where Democracy is being put at risk, and inherently, the current financial system.

The IMF has already come public about a Great Reset. Central banks are under tremendous pressure as debts are reaching worrying levels, and with the stress of technological deflation, the only solution the current system has is to continue printing money to keep the system alive.

I agree with Jared A. Brock when he says:

To be clear, the collapse of crypto coin prices is a very good thing. We need every single coin speculator to skitter off to other markets so Bitcoin and the rest can find long-term price stability at rational rates so they can function and truly compete with wildly corrupt national fiat currencies.

I'm investing in the stock market, but also in Bitcoin and Ethereum. I don't believe any of these systems will fall. But I think a new system is going to be created. Then, like the infinite game, governments, central banks, and developers and coders will find a system, part centralized, and part decentralized, that will serve humanity.

Money is the ultimate technology, and because of that, we need to find better ways to use it, especially for the two-thirds of the entire world population that hasn't got access to a banking account.

These cyclical periods of booms and bursts will keep happening. The first liquidity crisis occurred in the year 33 a.D. in the ancient Rome. Emperor Tiberius used the money to bail out banks and companies.

The last liquidity crisis happened in 2008, and the 9-page-white-paper was born and lead to the Bitcoin network and the blockchain technology.

El Salvador adopted Bitcoin as a legal tender. Some states in the US are buying Bitcoin to their balance sheets. The Fed announced plans for a white paper examining whether it should develop a digital currency of its own. Tesla and Square bought Bitcoin to their balance sheets. Goldman Sachs ramps up bitcoin trading in a new partnership with Mike Novogratz's Galaxy Digital.

At some point, the world is trying to find the best way to make the Bitcoin network an excellent financial solution to these endless financial constraints. Technology was always the tool humans used to find new alternatives to what was failing.

Now, central banks and governments are studying better ways to manage money in a cryptographic form as the world moves to total digitized format.

As Ollie Leech from Coindesk.com recently shared:

Google has partnered with multiple crypto-focused companies, become an enterprise network validator for Theta, a decentralized video streaming crypto project, and more recently added a dedicated "crypto" data tab to its finance page.

Microsoft launched an Identity Overlay Network (ION) built on the Bitcoin blockchain and filed a patent in 2020 for a crypto mining system powered by human activity.

Facebook famously announced its controversial Libra cryptocurrency in 2019 (it is now known as Diem and expected to be released sometime in 2021).

Amazon is planning to launch its own cryptocurrency project and recently announced its managed blockchain now supports Ethereum. In 2017, Amazon Technologies also purchased a number of cryptocurrency and Ethereum-centered domain names.

The truth is that the business world is trying to find bridges between analog ecosystems and the blockchain.

Those who are building the blockchain and the Bitcoin network are playing the infinite game because they create new and simpler forms of technologies that the analog world couldn't deliver in a fast, cheap, and decentralized way.

Developers and coders are not building new infrastructures to beat analog solutions. Instead, they create entirely new infrastructures under different premises to serve humans in a more just, fair, and individual term.

We're probably about to see 100 years of change in the next ten years.

The amount of technological disruption that was incremented by the pandemic, with so many behavioral economic shifts happening in this short period, will lead the world to another innovative boom where artificial intelligence and robotics will center all creations.

——————————— *NF* ———————————

Final Thought

I keep believing that Bitcoin is the most pristine store of value, but that's my personal belief.

I also believe that the current system will keep devaluing my time and energy by an ancient inflation tool.

If you study money history, you'll know that governments did devalue their currencies for centuries. That's the only way they can increase their spending at the expense of labor from those who pay taxes.

The system has always worked this way. I don't believe it will work any differently in the near future unless a decentralized protocol shows us a miraculous solution, which to this day, I still haven't been able to understand if it exists.

If we had already found a better solution to the monetary system, it would already be adopted, but the truth is that as much as I read about money history and also about the Bitcoin network, I still can't find a perfect solution to the monetary system. And I guess no one can.

What if, as Jeff Booth says in his book, instead of trying to stop deflation at all costs, we embrace it? That would mean we could get more for less. We would accept abundance, have most things for free as technology and robotic would allow it to happen. As a result, new industries would be created, and innovation would allow most people not to work anymore because it wouldn't be necessary.

It's hard to imagine a world like this, significantly because we all grew up in a world where these choices did not exist.

I don't even know if this world would work better than the world we live in today.

However, if technology keeps pressing the world's economy into a deflationary cycle, maybe this is the way things will happen.

You watch on national television economists talking about the UBI (Universal Basic Income). But you didn't listen to them talking about it ten years ago, did you?

So, the world is really changing, and we live in extraordinary times.

The infinite game of the Bitcoin network tells me this technology will change the world for the better. You may think otherwise. But one thing is for sure. Whatever we, as human beings, will achieve with these technological innovations will have to serve us better than the previous versions.

Welcome to the Exponential Age.

HOW ETHEREUM WILL RESHAPE AND TOKENIZE ENTIRE SECTORS OF OUR ECONOMY

In the Exponential Age, tokens and communities will dictate trends and abundance.

Ethereum is a supercomputer. Ethereum uses blockchain technology to decentralize every piece of technology or app you currently use.- Tim Denning in Medium.com

It should be easier to understand, but since Ethereum was created by developers and coders, the best thing you and I can have is their complex explanation.

Tim Denning did an excellent job by explaining what Ethereum is in an ordinary people's version.

If you go to ethereum.org, Vitalik Buterin's creation, it's explained that Ethereum is a technology that's home to digital money, global payments, and applications. The community has built a booming digital economy, bold new ways for creators to earn online, and so much more. It's open to everyone, wherever you are in the world — all you need is the internet.

Investopedia explains it better:

As a blockchain network, Ethereum is a decentralized public ledger for verifying and recording transactions. The network's users can create, publish, monetize, and use applications on the platform and use its Ether cryptocurrency as payment.

If you think Ethereum is a secret society of nerds living underground surrounded by powerful computers, you're not seeing things as they really are.

Today, young entrepreneurs are learning code to build their projects on the Ethereum blockchain. They only know digital, and when they have a platform with their own currency, Ether (ETH), their own ecosystem, and see every company desperately trying to understand its technology, they know better than anyone else where the future is being built.

And if you think young kids are the only ones running into this technology, they're not. **Google** has recently partnered with multiple crypto-focused companies and become an enterprise network validator for Theta, a decentralized video streaming crypto project. **Microsoft** launched an Identity Overlay Network (ION) built on the Bitcoin blockchain and filed a patent in 2020 for a crypto mining system. **Facebook** announced its controversial Libra cryptocurrency in 2019 and recently changed its name to Diem. **Amazon** is planning to launch its own cryptocurrency project and recently announced its managed blockchain now supports Ethereum.

Now think with me. If the most valuable companies in the world are shifting from the old Internet to Internet 3.0, this last one built in the blockchain ecosystem, where do you think the rest of the world's economy will shift to?

— *nF* —

All disruption starts with introspection.

In one of his presentations, Tony Seba, a lecturer in Entrepreneurship, Disruption, and Clean Energy at Stanford University, explained that in the 1900s, on the 5th avenue, a photo was taken showing the streets full of horses and carriages, and only one car circulating.

13 years later, on the same spot, on the 5th avenue, the same photographer took a picture. In a sea of cars, there was only one horse.

Now, if we talk about technology disruptions, and we try to forecast what the future may be 10 or 20 years from now, ordinary people like you and me have great difficulty visualizing new trends or new devices that will be part of our daily lives or even the type of vehicles we're going to drive.

However, just last week, Richard Branson took his first aerospace tourism trip.

Usually, what we do it's being very skeptical about the ability of human beings to produce new technologies, and for that reason, either we don't believe in them, or we believe that they will only appear 50 years from now.

However, if you hear all Tony Seba's presentations, you'll find a pattern in all technological disruptions. When we face an exponential era of technological innovations combined, like the one we're living in today, massive changes arise at the speed of light, without knowing how they could be created at such a speed.

Before the pandemic, few people knew what the Bitcoin standard or Ethereum blockchain was.

Robotics and artificial intelligence have been evolving under our radars. Machines have replaced some jobs, and we're seeing many of us working at home, not intending to return to our jobs, at least not in the same parameters that we used to.

So, having many entrepreneurs developing another kind of internet, where they are trying to reinvent the financial system as we know it, is just another technological disruption.

And what we see now is things like the CEO of a cryptocurrency brokerage having a meeting with the Chairman of the Federal Reserve. Meaning, Federal Reserve Chair Jerome Powell met with the chief executive of cryptocurrency exchange operator Coinbase Global Inc.

Central banks also want to understand the new technology. They know if they get skeptical and not doing anything, someone will surpass them. And the Bitcoin maximalists are trying to disrupt money, and by that, they have no doubt they want to eliminate commercial banks and central banks from the planet.

Bitcoin maximalists believe the financial system is corrupt, benefiting the few at the expense of the majority. And in fact, the system, intentionally or not, no longer meets the needs of the majority.

There is nothing better than a technological disruption to force everyone to rethink the system, redesign it so that new ways of creating money and circulating money can once again serve the interests of everyone, not just a few.

Ethereum and Bitcoin can be part of the solution.

———————————— *nF* ————————————

Education is not a problem. Education is an opportunity.

As I share my thoughts and knowledge about Bitcoin, Ethereum, and the blockchain, many readers criticize me, others congratulate me.

I see it as a good thing.

Critics make me reflect on what I write, the way I write, and some of them confront my way of seeing the world. Sometimes I agree with them and change my perspective about a particular subject. Other times I just confirm my convictions.

Most recently, I've been analyzing new blockchain projects, and a new world has arisen in front of my eyes.

One of them is LEDU, a decentralized learning ecosystem that teaches professionals and college students how to build genuine products. They are making the world's most extensive learning ecosystem for future technology topics such as artificial intelligence, cybersecurity, game development, data science, cryptocurrencies, and programming.

LEDU developed an education token (ERC20) that lives in the Ethereum blockchain. That means it can be bought, sold, or traded outside the ecosystem, just like any other cryptocurrency. Its value is going to be directly related to its success as a project.

More than 1 million educative professionals are already in this ecosystem, but they intend to expand exponentially. This token empowers a system of incentives that reward everyone that adds value to the ecosystem.

Learners can use education tokens to buy their subscriptions and donate to creators and engage directly with them. In return, learners will be rewarded with positive behavior inside the ecosystem.

Creators will also be rewarded with tokens. The more successful their projects will be, the more learners will pay for their services with tokens.

Even coders and developers can upgrade the educational system and be rewarded with tokens. Educational tokens will also be used for governance. Having tokens give voting power for users to vote in new upgrades and new services inside LEDU.

How do these tokens have value?

First, the LEDU token was designed to have as much utility as possible inside the platform. Meaning, as people keep using the platform, they'll keep needing tokens. As the demand of users grows, so does the demand for tokens. As a result, a percentage of tokens are burned at the end of each year, increasing the value of all remain tokens.

You can buy these tokens with BTC, ETH, or with a simple credit card.

LEDU wants to work directly with schools, libraries, and other online educational companies. Its mission is to be the major educational platform for creators to develop new projects.

———————————— *nF* ————————————

Final Thoughts

When Microsoft went public in 1986, most of its revenue came from selling software. Its competitors were IBM, AT&T, and Apple.

Microsoft was originally founded to write code for a company called MITS which produced the Altair computer.- thestreet.com

If Bill Gates and Paul Allen didn't develop their BASIC version and created MS-DOS, the Microsoft Disk Operating System, we probably wouldn't be here talking about one of the most valuable companies in the world.

Steve Wozniak, a self-educated electronics engineer, started to build his original blue boxes that enabled one to make long-distance phone calls at no cost. Jobs later told his biographer that if it hadn't been for Wozniak's blue boxes, there wouldn't have been an Apple.

I could be writing all day about little details that made the difference between the success or the complete disappearance of revolutionary companies.

Nowadays, we can make the same analogy to projects created in different blockchains, focusing primarily on the Ethereum platform.

There will be winners and losers. There will be protocols that win, others that no one will ever hear about again.

For technological disruptions to appear, vast amounts of money are always needed, usually in venture capital, but now also in a new format, with the tokenization of this new industry.

Any one of us can invest and believe in any protocol that is being developed on any blockchain. And just like SPACs or VCs, we could come away with highly profitable bets or with disheartening losses. Unfortunately, better formats have not yet been invented to finance significant technological changes.

But the tokenization of the economy seems to be a new trend, or can we already call it new financial engineering?

Nobody can predict the future. But as fervent observers, we can notice the signs that appear in front of our eyes.

The Internet of Things is here to stay. Clusters in Berlin, Singapore, and Miami are preparing themselves for the future of humanity. Maybe it's the innovation meccas, leaving Silicon Valley in the background.

Writing about innovation always leaves me with great curiosity because new things come out every day. There are no dull moments, no deserts to cross.

The Exponential Age has landed at our feet and will stay here for a while. It remains for us to observe, criticize, understand, and adapt to this new reality.

HOW TOKENS WILL BUILD POLITICAL ENLIGHTENING COMMUNITIES ALL OVER THE WORLD

How we can use blockchain to make politics better.

We always think everything is ok with politics until one day it isn't.

In Europe, the extreme right-wing continues to gain ground. In Portugal, we already have the extreme right-wing in Parliament. In Austria, the extreme right-wing already governs the country.

In the United States, we had Donald Trump completely dividing the country and instigate violence on Capitol Hill. In Brazil, Bolsonaro seems like a figure out of a comic book, claiming that the pandemic doesn't exist while thousands of graves are opened to bury the dead. If you really think that world politics is ok, start reading some news.

The wealth gap turns breeds more and more dissatisfaction and hopelessness, while central banks worldwide manage a vicious system that benefits the few, while the poor get poorer.

Sorry to make this intro with a dim view about politics, but we must be aware because we think it doesn't affect us until the day it does.

The complete financialization of the economy is changing the morality of politics, as more and more it has to do with money printing and debts, and less to do with productivity, companies, and ordinary people like you and me.

I've been studying innovation and technology for several years, and for those who are less aware of technological disruption, a new economy is being designed, 100% digital, decentralized, based on smart contracts, tokens, and communities.

Welcome to the blockchain network.

———————————— _nf_ ————————————

Meet the Man With a Radical Plan for Blockchain Voting.

A political theorist named Santiago Siri created a nonprofit startup, Democracy.Earth, to fix the world's broken politics with the help of the blockchain.

"We want to tokenize the like," Siri says.

Siri created a project that he calls "political cryptocurrency" — blockchain-generated tokens that users can spend as votes.

Siri dreams of a new kind of social media platform on which we spend "vote tokens" that can do anything, from electing politicians and passing referendums to enacting the bylaws of a social club or establishing the business plan of a corporation. It's Democracy by click.- wired.com.

The interesting thing about the blockchain is that the middleman is being replaced by protocols managed by code created by developers. And while these ecosystems have evolved to dematerialize various industries, the last of which is the finance industry, now new projects are turning to politics.

Do not undervalue the power of decentralization, as we already have countries like El Salvador, Tanzania, and Paraguay adopting Bitcoin as a legal tender. Change is really happening, and young citizens worldwide have already realized it, with the advantage of interpreting the digital language much better than Millennials and GenZ.

Users of Democracy.Earth's one-size-fits-all governance platform — code-named Sovereign — would have infinite flexibility to vote on any kind of topic or person, whenever they log on. In the Democracy.Earth future, every day will be election day, and the ballot will include anything that enough of us think should be there.- wired.com

When the Bitcoin network started to grow worldwide, many said it would be a Ponzi Scheme, a get-rich-quickly scheme, or another kind of critics. However, here we are, with Goldman Sachs close to offering bitcoin and other digital assets to its wealth management clients and the Wyoming state buying Bitcoin to its balance sheets.

At the same time, the Federal Reserve is studying the adoption of a cryptocurrency (some have already named it Fedcoin) managed by a CBDC (Central Bank Digital Currency). So, the change is happening in the financial world.

The question is about politics. When will politicians start to talk publicly about the necessity of moralizing politics with technological innovations that get it more transparent, stable, and democratic?

If the dream of bitcoin, the token generated by Satoshi Nakamoto's blockchain, was to free money from central bank control, then the dream of Sovereign is to free politics from central government control.- wired.com

In the following decades, we're going to witness a titan fight between total centralization and libertarian decentralization of everything.

Governments and central banks will use technology to complete the centralization of the monetary system, with the goal/illusion of avoiding future massive financial crises.

The blockchain and the Bitcoin network are designed to fight against central banks, using code and cryptography to solve economic constraints, building individual sovereignty for every human being on earth.

Between these two massive forces, something new will be created.

———————————— $\mathcal{NF}$ ————————————

Anyone that belongs to a party stops thinking.

The blockchain will not fix everything, for sure. But it's making a massive move into a more transparent way of building tokens and communities much closer to politics.

Another new project called Coalichain.io is a decentralized platform for liquid, accountable representation, and governance. It's a protocol based on Proof of Influence that converts participation in group governance into measure value.

Coalishain.io promises that representatives will carry responsibilities and stay away from any corruption. It also maximizes the security of votes without interruptions and impostors in a fully transparent process. It rewards users for their actions straight to their digital wallets, reduces the cost of elections, and maximizes flexibility for groups and organizational needs.

If you navigate through Coalichain.io, you'll find several videos that explain the protocol and the innovation tools.

$$\text{---} \mathcal{MF} \text{---}$$

Final Thoughts

If we're involved in the decision-making of a tokenized new system, we'll clearly know how our opinions were considered, and we can make our conclusions, moralizing the ecosystem in future elections.

These issues are not just being discussed, but most importantly, they are being redesigned in a decentralized system, putting this kind of discussion in a competitive mode now.

Meaning, the younger generations will obviously be more aware of these decentralized networks, use them, and finding new ways to materialize these digital tokens into their lives.

If new political ecosystems can be built where every voter can retain their tokens, citizens will feel more evolved in the decision-making process.

Most politicians complain about the difficult task of communicating with ordinary citizens; of course, they do. They work in a centralized system, where their decisions are far from making a real difference in every citizen's life.

I believe technology will give transparency to the political system, build a closer relationship between politicians and ordinary citizens, and open the fundraising system by tokenizing donations from billionaires and lobbyists.

We saw our lives benefit from the digitization of all mobile devices by Apple, the digitization of our social network by Facebook, the digitization of front-stores by Amazon, the digitization of libraries by Google. Yet, with flaws, the system improved, directly and indirectly, all of our lives.

The financial world is being digitalized as we speak. The political world will be next.

The Exponential Age is now a reality, with the Internet of Things being built to bring abundance and prosperity to all human beings.

I believe in the power of technology because tech is made by humans for humans. It only creates new tools to improve our quality of life. Technology was constantly developed to solve human problems.

We live in a world where the gamification is disrupting all sectors of the economy. Incentives are being built to create new infrastructures.

Show me the incentive, and I'll show you the outcome.- Charlie Munger

Humans will be the great beneficiaries of this new era. The destructive power of digital forces will win against the analog world. And it will be observed more fashionably in the following decades.

Robots will steal most of our jobs, but all-new industries will rise.

New monetary systems will have to be invented because most people on the planet will not need to produce anything. But they will build unique ecosystems to turn planet earth into a better place to live.

Consider this alternative: allowing abundance without the jobs might actually open an entirely new enlightenment era where we have time to enjoy the benefits that technology brings.- Jeff Booth in The Price of Tomorrow

A proper capitalist system can work well in an abundance environment because innovation is creativity, and creativity can build new needs, new ecosystems, new ways of living.

The deflationary force from technology is too great a force to be stopped. As much money central banks can create, they will not stop deflation from technological innovation.

The next great reset should contemplate deflation, where we could buy more with less. The Bitcoin network was built under that same premise. Unfortunately, however, central banks are working in the opposite direction.

Let us see if we can find an intelligent way to embrace abundance without too much damage.

To do that, we must understand the primary goal of technology: to create a better life for all human beings.

IT'S NOT THE CORPORATIONS THAT WILL HOLD THE POWER IN THE FUTURE, BUT COMMUNITIES OR TOKENS

The world will radically change and you better start changing your mindset too.

Last week I was having a coffee with several friends, and they tried to convince me that the Bitcoin network was a Ponzi scheme and the blockchain was entirely corrupted by hackers.

I was the only person trying to share my knowledge about the world of crypto. All my friends were rejoicing news, most of them fake, which appear in big letters in the prominent national newspapers.

That was further proof that the world is manipulated by the major corporations that belong to the big banks, which have strong links to governments. Those same governments have close connections to central banks.

Central banks, in themselves, feel threatened by this new technology that is becoming competition.

So, what do institutions and corporations do when they're threatened? They manipulate fake news and counter-information. In this case, they try to disallow technological innovation that, for the first time, is disrupting the most significant industry in the world-the money industry.

Remember what happened to the auto industry when Tesla started their Giga factories and massive electric vehicle production? That's it. They came with fake news.

Let's try to start with simple definitions to understand why communities and tokens will dominate trends and networks.

––––––––––––––––––– *nF* –––––––––––––––––––

What is the Bitcoin network?

In 2008 we faced a debt crisis that was known as the Great Recession. Banks collapsed, and the Federal Reserve and the European Central Bank had to bail out financial institutions to stop the burst.

Since then, the global economy has stayed in a recession only fueled by central banks through quantitative easing in a printing mania never seen before. Most experts are afraid of another monumental flop.

On 31 October 2008, a person or group of people named Satoshi Nakamoto created a 9-page white paper entitled: **Bitcoin: A Peer-toPeer Electronic Cash System.**

This document started with this statement:

A purely peer-to-peer version of electronic cash would allow online payments to be sent directly from one party to another without going through a financial institution.- Satoshi Nakamoto.

The story is almost romantic, as no one to this date knows who he, she, or they are. But what happened after this document was posted to a cryptography mailing list in the Internet network is outstanding.

The bitcoin network was created when Nakamoto mined the first block of the chain, known as the genesis block.

Spiked in the coinbase of this block was the text "The Times 03/Jan/2009 Chancellor on the brink of second bailout for banks."

That was the enigmatic message Nakamoto shared to the world, meaning by that of the instability caused by the fractional-reserve banking system.

Hal Finney was the receiver of the first bitcoin transaction in 2004 and had created the first reusable proof-of-work system. Finney downloaded the bitcoin software and received ten bitcoins on 12 January 2009 from Nakamoto itself.

Other cypherpunk supporters developed other infrastructures that came, ten years later, to give rise to one of the hottest financial markets.

Research produced by the University of Cambridge estimated that in 2017, there were 2.9 to 5.8 million unique users using a cryptocurrency wallet, most of them using bitcoin.- Wikipedia.

—————————————— *nF* ——————————————

What is the blockchain?

Blockchain is the record-keeping technology behind the Bitcoin network. It's a specific database in the way it stores information. Blockchains store data in blocks that are then chained together.

As new data comes in, it is entered into a new block. Once the block is filled with data, it is chained onto the previous block, making the data chained together in chronological order.- investopedia.com

There are different types of blockchains, but the most common ones are used as a ledger for transactions. Blockchains are immutable, which means that the data is irreversible.

In the specific case of the Bitcoin network, those transactions are permanently recorded and viewable to anyone.

A blockchain has a unique way of structuring the data, unlike a typical database. A blockchain collects information together in blocks.

Blocks have certain storage capacities and, when filled, are chained onto the previously filled block, forming a chain of data known as the "blockchain."- investopedia.com

Blocks are always stored chronologically and are added to the "end" of the blockchain. After a block is added to the end of the blockchain, unless the majority reach a consensus to do so, it's almost impossible to change.

That's why thousands of hackers tried to hack the system for decades and never succeeded.

—————————————— *nF* ——————————————

What is a cryptocurrency?

A cryptocurrency is a digital currency that is secured by cryptography. It's very difficult, almost impossible to counterfeit or double-spend.

Most cryptocurrencies are decentralized networks based on blockchain technology. Some of the best known are Bitcoin, Ethereum, Ripple XRP, Litecoin, NEO, and IOTA.

Each one of them has its own network protocol. A network protocol is a set of rules determining how data is transmitted between different devices in the same network.

———————————— *nf* ————————————

What is a token?

In the Blockchain ecosystem, any asset that is digitally transferable between two people is called a token.- coinhouse.com

Ethereum is the blockchain where almost every token is issued. A token can be a new project, a new protocol for a new cryptocurrency, or another digital asset.

Yet, for such a protocol to work, it takes many nodes replicating the blockchain, miners willing to validate transactions, developers to develop the protocol and create portfolios supporting it (coinhouse.com).

A friend of mine created a protocol called SavingCoin, wherein my hometown in Portugal. Then, he went to Cyprus to present it to investors, but the project didn't take off, and sixty thousand euros were lost.

Like in any other business, entrepreneurs try their luck; sometimes they win, sometimes they lose.

———————————— *nf* ————————————

What is an Alt-coin?

Altcoins are different protocols than Bitcoin.

The crypto world has been boosting with entrepreneurship and innovation. So, naturally, different kinds of coins were invented, some of them sharing the same characteristics as Bitcoin and new approaches.

Some Altcoins use different consensus mechanisms to produce blocks or to validate transactions.

Some of the Altcoins even distinguish themselves from Bitcoin, like the ones that provide smart contracts or low-price volatility.

As time goes by and technology evolves, new needs related to speed and security are required for this protocol type.

For example, Ethereum 2.0 was created to improve the network's security and scalability.

Ethereum 2.0 (ETH2) is an upgrade to the Ethereum network that aims to improve the network's security and scalability. This upgrade involves Ethereum shifting their current mining model to a staking model.-coinbase.com

———————————— NF ————————————

It's not the corporations that will hold power in the future, but communities or tokens.

We're entering an age of communities. And I'm going to give you an extreme example- **Dogecoin.**

In his tweeting mania, Elon Musk started to empower the crypto community, by his network influence, to invest in a cryptocurrency called Dogecoin.

Formed initially as a joke, **Dogecoin** was created by IBM software engineer Billy Markus and Adobe software engineer Jackson Palmer. … Markus had designed **Dogecoin's** protocol based on existing cryptocurrencies Luckycoin and Litecoin, which use scrypt technology in their proof-of-work algorithm. - Wikipedia.

Dogecoin reached a market capitalization of $85,314,347,523.

Seeing money as a trust protocol and money starting to be interpreted as a digital network protocol, you will see strange phenomena like Dogecoin, instigated by people like Musk, with a powerful network effect, impacting on prices of some of the most prominent cryptocurrencies.

This extreme example only suggests the power of the network effect.

People like Cathy Wood, Chamath Palihapitiya, or Mark Cuban have that network effect of making real change in people's mindsets.

We're entering an age of communities. It's not corporations that old the power anymore, but communities and tokens. It's a radical change in how the world works.

This network effect is going to be driven by token economics.

People are starting to realize the power they have to create unique communities around themselves and their businesses.

Tokens drive communities, because they take the right behavior structure. - Raoul Pal in Realvision.com

------------------------------ *nF* ------------------------------

Final Thoughts

Recently I wrote an article about the gamification of the future economy.

How about the tokenization of economics? We'll probably hear more of these terms in the future, as innovation occurs in the financial world.

Some states of the US arc already embracing these innovative ways of storing value. Most people don't believe or understand what's going on in the crypto world.

However, the change is here. Countries like the US and Canada, and at a smaller pace the European Union, are trying to embrace the digitization of the entire financial system.

Central banks and governments will try to do their best to stabilize the financial system. It's their job to do so.

Yet, a new way of looking at money and transactions have taken place. I believe in regulation, and for the stability of the financial industry, we need rules, not anarchy.

But rules made by humans, or code?

By humans, we already know what awaits us: more inequality and the gap between the rich and the poor. And from time to time, a crisis puts us all the poorest, without ground and hope.

Or, on the other hand, a cryptographic code being the simplest way to conclude contracts between two parties to exchange services.

Do we prefer the war between technological deflation and monetary inflation? Or are we all moving closer to a system that can really benefit everyone equally? All human beings in the world will have access to a system, not just the "chosen ones" from rich countries.

If the tokenization of economics wins the marathon, we're about to witness the complete disruption of the economy as we know it.

New communities will lead the way. Unused tokens will spread the tendencies and go looking for the money.

The fairest communities will win, create the best incentives, and make the world a more equal place.

Yet, even in this tokenization of the future economy, we will always need a leap of faith.

REFERENCES

1. We argue that Friedman's economic writings assume an economy in which businesses operate under limited liability protection, which allows corporations to privatize their gains while externalizing their losses. By accepting limited liability, Friedman must also view business as embedded in social interdependency, which serves as the logical and moral foundation for corporate social responsibility (CSR).- Ignacio Ferrero, W. Michael Hoffman, Robert E. McNulty in https://onlinelibrary.wiley.com/

2. Today, the Basel Committee on Banking Supervision issued a public consultation on preliminary proposals for the prudential treatment of banks' crypto-asset exposures. While banks' exposures to cryptoassets are currently limited, the continued growth and innovation in crypto-assets and related services, coupled with the heightened interest of some banks, could increase global financial stability concerns and risks to the banking system in the absence of a specified prudential treatment. - https://www.bis.org/

3. A purely peer-to-peer version of electronic cash would allow online payments to be sent directly from one party to another without going through a financial institution. Digital signatures provide part of the solution, but the main benefits are lost if a trusted third party is still required to prevent double-spending.- Satoshi Nakamoto in https://bitcoin.org/en/

4. Once bondholders determine that governments have little ability to repay or service the debt, the risk premium (or interest rates) on the debt will rise. Sure, governments can monetize and make their 24 currencies worthless, but as other central banks monetize as well, the strategy itself becomes irrelevant. Jeff Booth in https://www.amazon.com/s?k=The+Price+of+Tomorrow&ref=nb_sb_noss

5. The Great Reset agenda would have three main components. The first would steer the market toward fairer outcomes. To this end, governments should improve coordination (for example, in tax, regulatory, and fiscal policy), upgrade trade arrangements, and create the conditions for a "stakeholder economy." At a time of diminishing tax bases and soaring public debt, governments have a powerful incentive to pursue such action.- Klaus Schwab, founder and Executive Chairman of World Economic Forum in https://www.weforum.org/agenda/2020/06/now-is-the-time-for-a-great-reset/

6. If everything- not just phones or Internet companies but EVERYTHING- is giving far more performance and at the same time falling in price, a family that makes $75,000 this year and struggles to make ends meet could make $70,000 next year and the dollars would go further. And then $60,000 a few years after that and it would go further still, continuing to gain more for less with the natural deflationary trend in technology. That would allow us to step off the existing treadmill of chasing higher and higher prices, requiring even higher-paying jobs to keep up. That may sound radical, but if technology is deflationary, and we expect technology to continue its advance into more and more industries, it may not be radical at all. It may be the only sane thing to do.- Jeff Booth in https://www.amazon.com/s?k=The+Price+of+Tomorrow&ref=nb_sb_noss

7. If you think that secrecy from governments and no KYC is bitcoins future, you don't understand what adoption looks like. They will regulate it. You will declare it. You will have to do KYC, and that is fine. It doesn't take away its store of value but just integrates it.- Raoul Pal from https://www.realvision.com/

8. For example, if you don't understand how the Roaring '20s led to a debt bubble and a significant wealth gap, and how the bursting of that debt bubble led to the 1930–33 depression, and how the depression and wealth gap led to conflicts over wealth all around the world, you can't understand the forces that led to Franklin D.

Roosevelt being elected president. You also wouldn't understand why, soon after his inauguration in 1933, he announced a new plan in which the central government and the Federal Reserve would together provide a lot of money and credit, a change that was similar to things happening in other countries at the same time and similar to what is happening now. Ray Dalio on https://www.linkedin.com/in/raydalio/

9. The Metaverse: a persistent, live digital universe that affords individuals a sense of agency, social presence, and shared spatial awareness, along with the ability to participate in an extensive virtual economy with profound societal impact.- Piers Kicks on https://www.youtube.com/watch?v=NNG_dwHPoTQ&t=798s

10. Duolingo is an online language-learning app. It's pervasively and thoughtfully gamified: points, levels, achievements, bonuses for "streaks," visual progression indicators, even a virtual currency with various ways to spend it. The well-integrated gamification is a major differentiator for Duolingo, which happens to be the most successful tool of its kind. With over 60 million registered users, it teaches languages to more people than the entire US public school system.- Kevin Werbach, Associate Professor of Legal Studies and Business Ethics, Wharton School at University of Pennsylvania

11. When used carefully and thoughtfully, gamification produces great outcomes for users, in ways that are hard to replicate through other methods.- Kevin Werbach and Dan Hunter in https://knowledge.wharton.upenn.edu/article/for-the-win/

12. Gamification has long been applied to learning and marketing. Just think of how the military has embedded gaming techniques into its flight simulators. Today, businesses and marketers — especially in the consumer space — regularly employ gaming techniques. Gaming techniques, such as leader boards, simulations, challenges, "top scorers," and the like, are natural extensions of performancebased work. Additionally, Reward &

Recognition professionals are probably best positioned to both use and move this vital concept forward.- Dr. Michael Wu, PhD in https://theirf.org/research/game-mechanics-incentives-recognition/130/

13. The beauty of living in a renaissance moment is that we can retrieve what we lost the last time around. Just as medieval Europeans retrieved the ancient Greek conception of the individual, we can retrieve the medieval and ancient understandings of the collective. We can retrieve the approaches, behaviors, and institutions that promote our social coherence.- Douglas Rushkoff in https://medium.com/team-human/we-went-from-tribal-to-individual-something-else-must-come-next-abb5c090f766

14. We need to step back and reflect on how the great economic paradigm shifts in history occur. (…) There have been at least seven major economic paradigm shifts in history, and they are very interesting anthropologically because they share a common denominator. And that is at a certain moment of time three technologies emerge and converge to create what we call in engineering a general-purpose technology platform.- Jeremy Rifkin in https://www.youtube.com/watch?v=QX3M8Ka9vUA&t=3759s

15. In the 24 hours since this time yesterday, over 200,000 acres of rainforest have been destroyed in our world. Fully 13 million tons of toxic chemicals have been released into our environment. Over 45,000 people have died of starvation, 38,000 of them children. And more than 130 plant or animal species have been driven to extinction by the actions of humans. (The last time there was such a rapid loss of species was when the dinosaurs vanished.) And all this just yesterday.- In " The last hours of ancient sunlight " by Thom Hartmann - https://www.amazon.com/Last-Hours-Ancient-Sunlight-Revised/dp/1400051576/ref=sr_1_1?keywords=The+last+hours+of+ancient+sunlight&qid=1638817269_1

16. Experts have found a direct correlation between a nation's wealth and an adequate property rights system. This is because real estate is a form of capital, and capital raises economic productivity and thus creates wealth.- Loup Brefort, Country Manager for Serbia, The World Bank in https://www.worldbank.org/en/news/opinion/2010/11/18/Unlockin the-Dead-Capital

17. Large databases, advanced algorithms, inexpensive sensors, and all kinds of robotics will converge to face middle management's lucrative jobs. Any function that is predictable and routine will be a target for improving efficiency through automation.- John Pugliano in https://www.amazon.com/Robots-are-Coming-Profiting-Automation/dp/1612436692/ref=sr_1_1? keywords=Robots+are+Coming%3A+A+Human%E2%80%99s+S 1

18. If everything- not just phones or Internet companies but everythingis giving far more performance and at the same time falling in price, a family that makes $75,000 this year and struggles to make ends meet could make $70,000 next year, and the dollars would go further. And then, $60,000 a few years after that, and it would go further still, continuing to gain more for less with the natural deflationary trend in technology. That would allow us to step off the existing treadmill of chasing higher and higher prices, requiring ever-higher-paying jobs to keep up. That may sound radical, but if the technology is deflationary, and we expect technology to continue its advance into more and more industries, it may not be radical at all. It may be the only sane thing to do.- Jeff Booth in https://www.amazon.com/s? k=The+Price+of+Tomorrow&ref=nb_sb_noss

19. In the world of robotic precision, incompetence will not be tolerated. Whatever one's job function, the fundamental quality standard will be competent execution of the task. Feedback from data exploration, cloud computing, and social media will instantly

assess the performance of all jobs.- John Pugliano in
https://www.amazon.com/Robots-are-Coming-Profiting-Automation/dp/1612436692/ref=sr_1_1?
keywords=Robots+are+Coming%3A+A+Human%E2%80%99s+S
1

20. You have an asset and a monetary network that it's able to achieve cash finality anywhere in the world, at any time, at no variable cost.- Jack Mallers in https://www.youtube.com/watch?
v=7rExf6EKHW4

21. Critics of QE (Quantitative Easing) quickly claimed that money printing would produce a wave of inflation on this scale. Inflation never came because inflation has little to do with money supply per see. Inflation is a psychological phenomenon based on expectations and a form of adaptive behavior described mathematically as hypersynchronicity. From 2008 to 2018, that catalyst was missing because consumers were saving, paying off debt, and rebuilding their balance sheets.- James Rickards in https://www.amazon.com/Aftermath-James-Rickards-audiobook/dp/B07SRCT7GL/ref=sr_1_1?
crid=2Q6ESQ0INIYS7&keywords=aftermath+james+rickards&qi
1

22. Some commentators argue that financial institutions are not doing enough to stop money laundering and are instead filing SARs to protect themselves from criminal prosecution while profiting from processing suspicious transactions.-
https://www.jdsupra.com/legalnews/fincen-files-highlight-prevalence-of-68053/

23. The OCC supervises nearly 1,200 national banks, federal savings associations, federal branches, and foreign bank agencies that 112 conduct approximately 70% of all banking business in the United States. The OCC's mission is to ensure that national banks and federal savings associations operate in a safe and sound manner, provide fair access to financial services, treat customers fairly, and

comply with applicable laws and regulations.-
https://www.occ.treas.gov/about/index-about.html

24. The estimated amount of money laundered globally in one year is 2– 5% of global GDP, or $800 billion — $2 trillion in current US dollars. Due to the clandestine nature of money laundering, it is however difficult to estimate the total amount of money that goes through the laundering cycle.-
https://www.unodc.org/unodc/en/money-laundering/overview.html

25. As legitimate cryptocurrency use goes up, crypto crime as a percentage goes down. 2020 crypto crime was down 57% from 2019, dropping from $4.5 billion to $1.9 billion in 2020.-
https://ciphertrace.com/2020-year-end-cryptocurrency-crime-and-anti-money-laundering-report/

26. To be clear, the collapse of crypto coin prices is a very good thing. We need every single coin speculator to skitter off to other markets so Bitcoin and the rest can find long-term price stability at rational rates so they can function and truly compete with wildly corrupt national fiat currencies.- Jared A. Brock in
https://survivingtomorrow.org/bitcoiners-are-desperate-for-one-last-pump-so-they-can-dump-31f2e58d7025

27. Google has partnered with multiple crypto-focused companies, become an enterprise network validator for Theta, a decentralized video streaming crypto project, and more recently added a dedicated "crypto" data tab to its finance page. Microsoft launched an Identity Overlay Network (ION) built on the Bitcoin blockchain and filed a patent in 2020 for a crypto mining system powered by human activity. Facebook famously announced its controversial Libra cryptocurrency in 2019 (it is now known as Diem and expected to be released sometime in 2021). Amazon is planning to launch its own cryptocurrency project and recently announced its managed blockchain now supports Ethereum. In 2017, Amazon Technologies also purchased a number of

cryptocurrency and Ethereum-centered domain names.- Ollie Leech in https://www.coindesk.com/business/2021/03/04/is-apple-buying-bitcoin-separating-facts-from-fiction/

28. Microsoft was originally founded to write code for a company called MITS which produced the Altair computer.- Eric Reed in https://www.thestreet.com/technology/history-of-microsoft-15073246

29. Siri dreams of a new kind of social media platform on which we spend "vote tokens" that can do anything, from electing politicians and passing referendums to enacting the bylaws of a social club or establishing the business plan of a corporation. It's Democracy by click.- https://www.wired.com/story/santiago-siri-radical-plan-for-blockchain-voting/